Autobiography

of a

Poet

Dan Brady

Volume Three

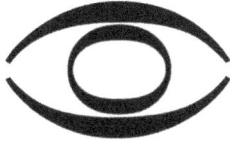

One Insight Press

ISBN 13: 978-0-578-64538-4
ISBN 10: 0578645384

One Insight Press
San Francisco, CA

Please see my author's page on Amazon.com
https://www.amazon.com/author/dan-brady

Foreword!

Welcome to the portals of the past, mazes of memory, the reservoir of reflections, the quilt of quietude, the translucent wash of wonders, and profound seasons of silence.

Dan

See? Here I am at three months.

Introduction:

This autobiographical collection was partly inspired by my age, 67 this past year. The process of assembling the manuscript provided enough sadness and joy to give me a mental and emotional work out. I did notice gaps, events and circumstances important enough to be included but which I've never written about, however, I wanted to keep this simple – deciding to use only pieces I already had. The collection is organized in chapters according to periods of my life, the pieces reflecting or representing my experience. Some pieces are based on memories, some on reflections, even workshop prompts, while others, mainly those later on, were written concurrent with the events or circumstances they are meant to portray. There are some pieces appropriate to more than one section. There are poems about friends, significant events, or internal dialogues, thoughts, and revelations. You may note stylistic variations, which may be because I kept older poems formatted as they were. You may note words or phrases in parentheses; I do this to indicate the presence of homonyms I wish to reference. I've also enjoyed the luxury of including leisurely prose pieces. I hope you'll enjoy the journey, find something of use, and, as with all of my books, pass it along.

Dan

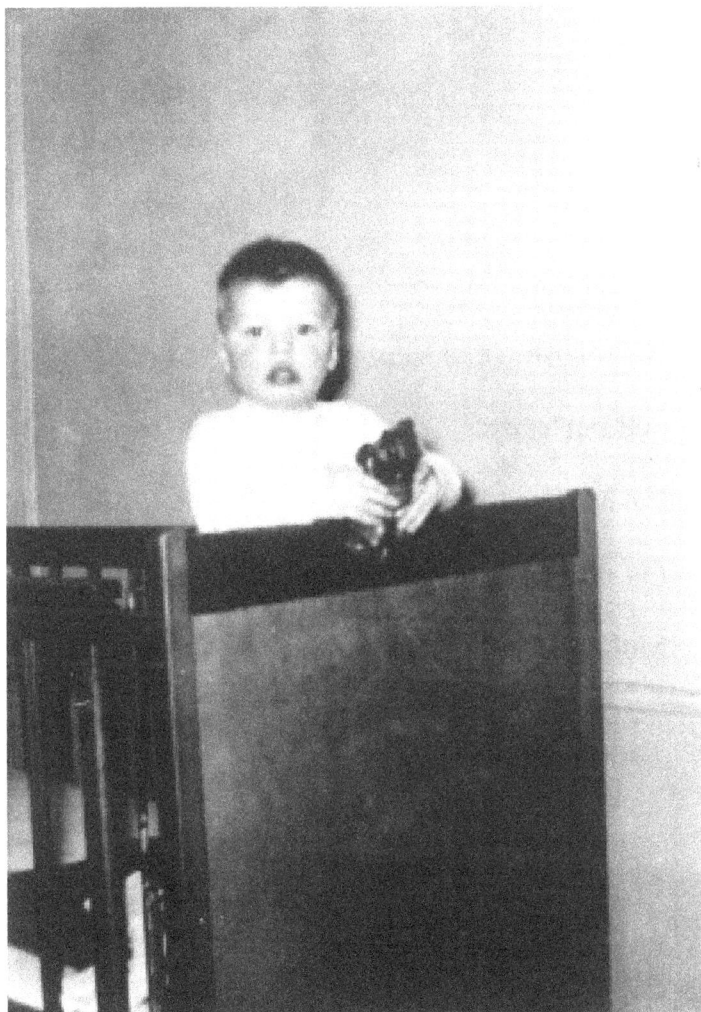

This picture is, maybe, a year or so later.

Table of Contents   Volume Three

Chapter Seven   **1 to 121**
97/12 – 11/8   **University St.**

I was full time teaching as Wendy and I managed the usual ups-and-downs of life, not to mention the passing of family members and friends.

Chapter Eight   **122 to 223**
11/8 – present   **30th Avenue**

I went to open mics, began hosting Sacred Grounds, retired from teaching, and began to publish prose and poetry.

In Volume One

I was born August 16th, 1952 in New York City. I was the forth born of seven children.

After Dad died, my Mom moved us from New York City to Fremont California. She had been born in or near Sacramento.

This was only a four-year stretch but it was the first time I was truly on my own working odd hours as an orderly in a facility caring for elders. I learned how to make ends meet. For a time I lived on Jules Avenue, where I first self identified as a poet. This was also when I began working full time.

I continued working full time and writing. I was, for the most part, a reclusive person and enjoying quantities of solitude.

In Volume Two

During this time I lived in the inner sunset of San Francisco.
I became more involved with writing and learned a great deal,
began to publish, attend open mics, and connect with the
Theosophical Society where I established several important
friendships.

Writing was put aside for a few years because teaching
took up a great deal of time and married life became vitally
important to me. By the early 90's I began going first to
haiku and then open mic poetry events.

****
Chapter Seven

97/12 – 11/8   **University St.**

I was a full time teacher, confident and capable. I provided trainings, mentored younger teachers, went to various meetings, contributed voluntary efforts to my school and was very interested in, challenged by, and involved with education.

Notably Wendy and I were learning how to cope with life stressors, deaths in the family, moving, and challenges of various kinds. We managed to find happiness, however, our heart-felt love was ever our sweet redoubt.

During this time I became involved with the poetry scene in San Francisco. I explored it and found Sacred Grounds about the year 2,000. Eventually, I created an open mic calendar, several volumes of print on demand books, and attended Sacred Grounds while Jehannah Wedgwood was still the host. During this time, when my career had difficulties, due to incompetent managers and systemic chaos, I began planning to retire, which I did in 2014.

The child I once knew
First boyfriend in one hand
A basketball in the other

2

<u>*One*</u>

Relationship and Romance

A stroll
About our neighborhood
The sidewalk was   lightly shaded
A sprinkle of dusky rain
In fresh   moving air

I passed a dark silken scarf
Strewn gracefully – along – by a driveway

But I continued … then there came … a moment
Of perfume
I thought of the scarf – looked back
But it was downwind

Another waft … this … warm, musky
Followed by another … floral
Sweet … and then … something else
As I glanced about

The near garden was flowerless
The trees – all barren of branch – and the wind
From down the way and quickening to blusters
Was clean   the sky,
Occluded by a layer of misshapen clouds,
Was heavily dark

So … I … wondered
A moment … stood but … nothing more
Nostrils drew in cool clean air   and

    I thought of you

        I was so glad   thankful

            Just … to be   thinking o

Here we are visiting friends in the lovely Portola neighborhood, of San Francisco – beautiful!

Some Day

There's a woman that I know
She's turning sixty-one
Came out here from down in old Virginia
Flew to San Francisco … on silver wings and dreams
And we said someday … we'll go dancing on the moon

But my friends they could not see her
For she's was very like the breeze
And seemed far too different in their eyes
But I, I held her to me, and kept her hand in mine
We said someday … we'll go dancing on the moon

And sure we have our stormy days
But those bright ones – they come right along
We've kept our love together – so it stays – strong

So blow the winds of fortune
Or Gabriel's gold horn
We say someday … we'll go dancing on the moon

And yeah we have worn baggage
That we keep 'cuz we can't let it go
But we forget it all when we go dancing

She loves her old folksong tunes
As much as I … my muse
We say … someday … we'll go dancing on the moon

Oh the gleams of dreams twinkled in her eyes
As we gazed on our honey moon
And I know that our dance – well, it won't end soon
And I … I will hold her to me, and swing her just for luck
Laughing oh someday we'll go dancing on the moon

Inspiration Point

The Pacific off of Ocean Beach was beautifully calm
The sky above was almost clear
There was a slight haze, something of a breeze
It was Christmas Eve

If I could compose perfectly enough
To encompass this sight
Distant surfers bobbing in the blue gray waiting on a wave
The broad beach at a once-a-year minus tide
The people meandering
The lone yellow kite way to the south
The skittering Snowy Plover
The couple writing their nonsense words in the sand
Laughing

The black lab chasing waves

If I could take all this in then press it
Reducing it to a scrap of paper and proper scribble
It would be the last poem I would write

If I could have you see her eyes
And how winter's light played on them
How they hold every little thing
If you look carefully enough
It would be the last poem I would write

When we went out to the ocean's very edge
To watch water slide over the sand
Such a thin, thin layer – and how each grain glistened
As slips of water flowed back to the great mother
As the silvered gleam of tumbling crests
Row on row advanced
How plumes of spray splashed up   off Seal Rock

If I could have you hear the questions
Understand my fascination
How childhood memories of an ocean far away
Long, long ago   touched my baby toes
It would be the last poem I would have to write

I would be relieved of this
And serve no more the muse

But   when she just walked into dance
Careless and causeless
Clueless and wondering all the same

If I could have you see her smiling toward the sun
At just the right moment
A moment I'll never forget   well
If I could do any one of these simple things
It would be the last poem I would write

Life flows with currents unseen
A hand held
A whisper caught
A made up word
A wish for another day

How simple   a walk on the beach
If I could but tell you
And know that I had done well by you
By her in that telling
It would be the last poem I would write

Longing, Spelled Out

In your eyes   I   saw
So much   that one night
There was the moon
In its crescent phase
With Jupiter off to the left
And   there was
Orion's belt   glittering
Just below
The slight galactic haze

It was   all in there

As we embraced … and
Our heart's beat
One with the other's
And there were whispers'
Warm breath
Gracing our cheeks,
And how
Lips touching
Barely   at first
Slowly then   found the nape

Oh …   the soft
Fingers   twined
Silly   I know   but

It was   joyful

This then   is when I
Forever
Fell in love
With time

9

Everything, Everything

Though love does abide, this revival set us aglow
As sweet spring air freshened in from our window.

So above us motes, caught in slant light, were carried out
As below, in idyll, embraced, we found certain redoubt:

You abed beside me with our timely spirit
Replied to this life, deciding thus, to cheer it.

When, at rest, in disarray, tumbled thoughts came to mind
We spoke through a sigh, declaiming our common bind.

So those loose languorous afterglow dreams went awing,
Rose with our wishes lofting up to clouds for a fling!

Oh, set aside, the simple little mind and its torturous plays,
And part those fanciful curtains onto love's yesterdays!

Where oe'r spread are those pastoral scenes of storybook lore
Wherein everyone happ'ly dwells, peaceful, for evermore

Wedding night
   As we undress   birdseed scatters   all over
      The tiled floor!

November Is Silver

It was late in the afternoon
As we drove west on Lincoln
The sunlight glazed the windshield

Ordinary, enough, but a reflection not lost upon me,

With our windows down
We took in hints of brine and pine, and rain fresh green,
In the warm bouquet of Indian Summer air.

My wife and I going to Ocean Beach for a walk.
We parked, then carried out the old blanket.
About halfway to the surf, she chose a spot
Where we spread it out.

She lay down wanting just to get off her feet, rest,
Hear the surf and feel the light breeze.

I went to stand at the very edge of the ocean,
To get so close I'd see only the sky and water.
Quaintly, there was a haze,
Which gentled the distances into oblivion.

Out to sea a large freighter plied its way to China,
On a calm blue horizon
Nearer in the water was green brown, fertile,
The rich upwelling, again,
Ordinary, enough, but a reflection not lost upon me.

Closer in, where the lines of waves formed up
And breakers, in lively chaotic tumult, crushed one another
Tossing myriad flecks to glint and gleam
Each bright as any lucky dime
A shimmering field

And yes, it was silver,
All of it silver
And so bright
Though couldn't look upon it long
And its after image persisted.
I would glance back, again and again,
Just to see its simple majesty and mystical tint.
Sometimes, near where I stood,
The water would sweep in
A centimeter deep,
Limned with a foam and clear.

Ordinary enough, but a reflection not lost on me.

Yet – I knew she was standing behind me,
Before she spoke,
I'd "heard" a silence
In the ambient tapestry of the sound,
Knew she'd stopped, knowing I knew,
And when, after a moment, I turned,
As if to answer her unspoken question,
She mutely stepped to my side and held me to her
And so together we looked out.

Ordinary enough, but a reflection not lost upon me.

I cast a sidelong glance to her,
The waning sun's light had her face a blushing, golden tan,
Years younger, childlike new.
Her eyes were closed and she was half smiling.
Naught but dreams, I knew.
Far up the beach
The setting sun's light was awash prismatic on the sand,
Rich stretches of shimmering gold,
Vermilion, and velvety purple colors ran
As they changed places and shape

As the waters swept over the sand
And slipped back into the sea
Simply content, yet watchful,

So we'd not inundate our shoes
And smelling the salt air,

Ordinary, oh, yes, but a reflection not lost upon me,

Though something more of course
Something in all of this:

I took her hand and, as if by chance,
Holding it, I had her pulse,
And there was the ocean's tempo,
The setting sun's touch to the horizon,
The flapping of a kite,
The laughter of a stranger,
And when her hand replied to mine
I looked into her hazel eyes
There, there was the golden sun,
And a vast ocean of silver, in but its twinkling

All so ordinary, yes,
But, in reflection, nothing at all was lost upon me.

In the choir
   After chocolate rabbits
      We all hit the low notes

This is from a family 4th of July gathering in 2000 at Charlie's place in Fremont. It was huge; with a Hawaiian style roast pig, some 60 people, a stage, music, impromptu bands, and more!

This is Mom at that same event.

My oldest brother, John, and his wife, Sally, were in on that celebration. I do not have many photos save these few, which are of my immediate family members.

Our Twentieth

I remember you
That day these decades hence
Was it on a late August afternoon?
But you'll recall –
The inner sunset's sky was clear
And the breeze, though slight, was cool
Before you saw me; I'd seen you
Walking toward me with a long time friend
She introduced us, not by name, at first
Instead, she eyed me, "Look what I've found for you!"

We laughed and that was the start of it all
Between you and I   I don't remember
But we must have walked back the way I'd come
Because we stood on a couple squares of sidewalk
And talked for hours
Oh, maybe we shifted around now and again –
But we memorialized them some years later.
During our stay friends came and went
And the weather changed as high fog swept the sky away
And your smile, my dear, was dear
I hadn't gone to the Joe Miller walk that particular Thursday
Had I done so I would have met you there
I recall that I'd had a lunch date
Though I don't recall the person or why they never showed
So I'd gone on some errands in the neighborhood
Then headed down Ninth Avenue toward Golden Gate Park,
Which was where I met you walking along with Cienne

As we begin our 20th celebration
We're taking a week for our day
We began it with a fine dinner
Starting with a delicious dhal soup – the best in town
We shared our entrées, as is our custom but

There came a time when I saw you … close your eyes
Even as you seemed to look forward … and upward slightly
And, for a still, quiet moment … you were … intense
Your face as smooth with peace as if in sleep
But there was a whisper of a blush
Then a hint of a smile … a sigh one could easily miss
So … when your beautiful eyes opened
You wanted to explain

How it was because this man had been so polite … kind
The waiter so caring, someone else had smiled or chuckled
That a peculiar light glowed on a woman's grand face
And how the place became discretely colorful all at once
As you spoke your hands fluttered at your heart
As you speculated about a light, joyful, airy sense
And yes, the food had been … excellent
Then you said you loved my smile,
Which had me smile more broadly

Ah, what a time it was
So I took you hands in mine my dear
And told you your hands have not lost a bit of their warmth
Their soothing smoothness
Nor had my enjoyment of their touch diminished

Later that night,
We watched the Marx Brother's – A Day At The Races
Although we forgot to make the popcorn
We did not forget
To look into each other's eyes, kiss,
And proclaim our love
Between those times we did laugh

2

The next day, we're took in Shakespeare

But we do like our Shakespeare and was performed outside
And the actors spoke to the crowd
Using their naked voices in a beautiful amphitheater
We'd thought a picnic … or going out or
Letting the day decide us
We went off to Ocean Beach
Where we were to make sand castles
Write love letters in the sand
And laugh at waves as they came rollicking in
To take them all away

When we got there it was a beautiful day
We decided on dinner
Yes, we were served aromatic rice
Beautiful coconut milk soup, Thai style

Our waitress was gentle and poised
Even down to her fingertips

But the satisfaction was ours
Our smiles said it all   and we let each other know
Through our "bird whistles"
Our secret signs and security codes

The strand we strolled was at low tide
The silvered waters shown with a winter light's brilliance
And the scattering of people was comforting
Children played in the sand
Dogs bounded into the surf
And strollers read our passages
We wrote "forever" in the sand and in absolute terms
We made a sun on the horizon radiant
Drew inside it our hearts and a candle
Nearby we make a small castle

With a moat, surmounted with kelp
We stood back took in the sea's breath
And slowly left all those treasures strewn
For those passing to see or to tread upon with disregard
And you did dance a bit – ankle deep in the waters
Your delicate motions
Silhouetted in the shimmering silver wash
Of the foamy tumult as the waves washed ashore

3

We chose to relive our dreams
Such as we might
With deep reflections of twenty years
We stood on both of our onetime doorsteps
Sat where ghosts now must abide as memories might
Wished ourselves back to our longing and dreams
As we quietly we conferred
Before leaving off those old thresholds
Before taking to our slumber
A string of adventures
Both cute and endearing
Were what I recalled as my lids closed

4

We journeyed to our own dawn's place
Saw where I first saw you in your gown
Stood beneath the near redwoods brightening
Saw the patina of the slate tiles on the roof
The well crafted log work of the lodge
We prayed in its garden,
Explored a new and old path
We read a reprise
Those very words we spoke to each other back then and there
And we stood where we once stood

Spoke even of the dead ... the dear
Looked at our album, shared memories – the wedding cake
Tasting it, again, after a fashion
Saw Mikey at the strawberries
How everyone was so young ... everyone
From a time so long ago,
Temporal things all considered,
That it took my heart's breath away

5

We went south for a day
Stayed in a new fangled past
Tangled in our sheets
We played   had a romp
Slept deliriously
Ate far to well
Tipped way to much,
But ladies, I'll tell you, Rich was a waiter's waiter
Nearly perfect in execution
And we played our role
It was our tourist night out
We were heavenly and gay
On the beach
After we parked the car
We heard the sound's rhythm
Birds calling unseen
And our whispers,
Warm to our ears, spoke only of love

6

Then, returning, I marveled
At how we became exactly ordinary
How the inundation of the usual was soon upon us –
Even as we drove home the point seemed obscured

And we lost our way, in a manner of speaking,
Then, when we were home, there were messages
Our appointments or assignments
Both self-assigned or promissory to keep
But these did not preclude our memoir's gift
The rosy blush upon your breast … your smile
And giggle … the way you could jiggle … just so
We have enough love for the both of us it seems
And still, after these years
Times of plentitude

7

Yet our agenda was not complete
We went to the Palace of Fine Arts
You found the way to the very set of trees
And that perspective we'd had
From the embankment where we'd picnicked years ago

We sat under their shade
Took pictures and had ours taken
I tell you now
If I had the thousand words for each of them
There would not be enough
By any stretch of the imagination
And we took our time to stroll
Quite literally …
Along memory's lane

Now, it did take us time to find the other place
Where Mikey first touched toe to the Pacific
You knew the way to "carry our sleigh"
While I doubted your recall
And could only offer conflicting memories,
Which you accepted, calmly,
And with great understanding –

And brought us right to where we had been
Without saying a word
Nor did you smile ever so sweetly whilst saying
"I told you so."

8

I guess within such are the keys
Patience
Understanding
Serenity when under duress ... then forgiveness
And the inexpressible conviviality
That makes love over into something
That is nothing like anything else
In this wonder filled world of ours
And it is my fortunate circumstance
To report on that simple fact
With the hope that you'll investigate yourself
And bear witness to its verity

We yet harbor ours
For long these many years
And although we may not look like it, especially,
We are the wonders of happiness
We dreamt of

Our love is ever present
A gift, of course,
Which we offer every day
Without alteration
Without concern for a result
Or consequence

We bear it – opening ourselves
To its wonder and grace

Finally

I tell you someday
We'll be happy
Living a life that leaves us whole
Taking again those vows we made
All those years and years ago
For what they were and are
Now

Someday we'll be happy
With enough, just enough
To have some extra to share
To help when help is needed
To give when the giving is right
To answer whenever we're called to a bedside
To a hospice
To a friend in need

When it is that someday
And the holidays come round
And the feast is laid upon our table
And the sideboards boast
Of handpicked pride
Of timeworn recipes
Of precious china handed down cracks and all
Or an old time punch bowl
Or cards from those whose dear names
Are ever spoken of with regard and love

Someday … when we've made our home
And it has, in turn, made us
Someday we'll have the kind of kindness
Which our eyes will delight in showing
Through which we cherish our small contribution
To the Love of this world

When we have been laid out
When the mourners and singers come
And we, in our rest, are spoken of both lightly
And tearfully

It will be that someday when we'll look back
On the long wild ride our love has taken us on
All the woes we worried up
The sores we pressed into one another
As well as the blessings we dressed our wounds with
So that someday ... someday

When it is our turn
To stand in waiting before that glorious gate
We will find ourselves to be
No less ... and no more
Than we are now

And we'll recall how this day, now
Is some yesterday's someday
Just as the day we met
Was the someday we both dreamt of
For some long, long time before it dawned

And someday ... someday can be any day
Reflections being what they are
Love being what it is
Not to mention life
When bringing us to any new day
Reminds us that someday
Is any day we happen to be happily ever after

Turning And Planting *(After LAMA, 1995)*

Turning and planting this morning
Hand tilling in the old beds – life is stirred –
Worms turn up, gleaming, insects, in a daze apparently,
Crawl, hop, and buzz about bumping into things
When she calls from our window.
We talk over the garden.
She says, she "wants to make the bed" and smiles.
I say, "OK."
Then add, slyly, "but only because you're 'in a hurry.' "
A reference to our lapse this morning
When we'd forsaken business as usual for, well, business.
We'd both been taken away – I guess
I was thinking
She'd seen how we'd left the blankets and garments
Loosely distributed – one would say, carelessly, strewn
Breakfast, had been slow and dreamy
She'd made the oatmeal and I the French toast.
We had music on
As steam curled up in a sunbeam
My coffee mug – warmed my hands
Everything was done slowly, quietly
So we'd both forgotten what we'd left in our wake.

Early that morning   the glow
From just over the horizon,
Was filtered through our eastern windows
Gleamed golden through the frosted glass panes
Of the French doors
Separating the living room from our bedroom
It cast a warm amber light
So the beige wooden floor had a glow – as if newly waxed
And the room's ruddy brown wood trim
Seemed to have more than a touch of rosy light
As if newly painted

We marveled at the radiant transition
I saw her face in this magical light
And when her whisper had me smile and our hands met
And, cheek to cheek and laughed
Well, that's how it all got started.
We wound up more than slightly delayed
In setting our feet to the floor
We dallied, that's the word for it,
Refreshing ourselves in the luxury of romance.

So, later, when we talked over the garden,
And again, as we arranged the bedding
Lofting it up so as to let it waft down
We noticed – the lighting had changed again
It was both cooler and brighter,

That November morning … I saw you – peaceful and radiant
Smiling as if everything was new
And in the subtle winter light
Your face glowed from within and without
I was inspired. I went forth … only to return quickly
Bringing the best of the strawberries
We marveled at their numerous seeds
As we placed them onto each other's tongues
A simple luxury
Just as taking a moment for us
To relish their taste in a kiss
One might call this joy – most would call it love
As we sat, abed, tasting fruit and kisses
In what everyone would call a room
But which we called our "music box"
Because it was where we played,
Sang and danced together betimes
Where we came to understand
How, even in silent reverie, at rest, and in peace
We could hear the music of the spheres.

Still pond
In reflection   fireflies
Circle the moon …

On the phone, worlds apart,
You say, "It's the same moon."
As I touch the cold pane

This recent photo
Does nothing but injustice
Why even smile?

Her hands shake
Dropping the letter – faded photo
Her new   old tears

This was created from a prompt, the nature of which is clear from the content of the poem. It was roundly hailed as the best from that workshop. I included it because, well, we did have our ups and downs, but I had no other poem to represent that aspect of things.

The Argument

It can be a word,
A question, some bit of chaos,
It does not have to be much at all
To set the charge,
Strike flint to the flash
And fire a lightening line
Then thunders roll,
We let the dark beasts tear our hearts free
Their release, a cruel overflow
And suddenly,
Cataracts of insults vomit toward each other
Neither able to hold back
Neither can we shore up the facades
We face each other with
And so these props are cast aside
And the staging becomes method, a free for all
But the script is cast in stone for all that –
Venomous vocabulary
Slaps cruelty in our faces
Sarcasm pulls our masks askew
Our make-up runs
As sneering lips give mock smiles and,
Though the hands wring, we are wrought
Of what we fought
And we face off
Incompetent, we both push

Unable to hold our centers
And becoming bewildered, besieged,
We both bite for blood
Get nose to nose
With thoughtlessness rending each other
And in this darkening downpour
Our waxy faces melt tears of rage, sorrow, and remorse

We bring the storm to our own iron gates
And gather the mobs,
The witnesses we each call to our cause,
Who hurl our insults from their lips
Accusing, recriminating, quoting
We parry and thrust with sharp lies and cruel jests
But then, truly, it seems, only to nick and cut –
Despite the horrid gusto
For are we not still human?
Even in this extreme?
Do we not still care for each other?
And are we not still in love?
Oh yes, and then some
To be sure
To be sure.
We are in love, and then some.

30

Two

Self Portraits

Remembrance

Old songs ... memories
Yeah, those ones
When driving along
With time and distance to go
When the static begins to wash
In and out of your reception
So ... you hit a button
And on the new station
As clear as can be, and in but a few bars, a couple cords
You are back ... years ... decades
To one place ... one time ... one event
You can smell the roses
Feel the wind
Hear the rain
Know what is coming next
What you will say
What was said
What you've always wanted to add
So as to say what you really meant
And ask that question – just to check – to be sure
To see into a glance, understand the comment
Revisit the regret at not choosing the high ground
Or following the path untaken
To offer something
That would let understanding ... happen
To ask for forgiveness
To shrug off pride ... yes
Yes ... I know time travel
Speculation
What I would do all over again ... if I could

We are not forever young and for good reason
The river of time moves ever on
Struggle ... reach and grasp at the ring ... as we might

Hoping for respite ... pause ... time out
Wild eyes in the belief that this will help
But we never, ever get that chance
And we never will – that's the way it works
It's what we have to deal with
The be all and end all

No matter how much we deny it
Pray, beg ... wrench our hearts
Wring our souls   or dream on
We can never change what was – only our perception of it
Only, maybe, learn the lesson
And so change what we may yet do to amend

Know that your legends live on   your loves tell
Your script remains in record

Diamonds may be forever
And Gibraltar may crumble and fall
There may be blue skies over the white cliffs of Dover
And we'll remember the Roseville fair
So long ago
So long ago but you still remember

You can wave good-bye my friends
Let your sheaves fly unbound to the wind
And their leaves to scatter in flocks
Which then settle in the big muddy
To drown in brown of the past in its flow
To the ever-moving present
Let go and let life move   yes, cry no more
Yes, wish no more   and reflect not
And so love this life as you would no other
As if it were unique
And never ending

All day   one cricket
Over the fields   at dusk
Another joins in

Pine tree campground
In the deep dusty tire's track
A toddler's footprints

Near the hopscotch game
Last day of school   ice cream puddle
Captures a paper airplane

Daniel *(This pair, written at an art retreat, for a self portrait and then something combining Poe and Lovecraft.)*

1) The portrait

A smile accustomed to laughter,
Green eyes twinkling with wit,
The yellow sunlight of summer
In his careless, windblown hair
A laugh as if there was nothing that had to be done –
Or better to do
Than enjoy a picnic of silliness
And simply "be there" forgetting everything:
All the yesterdays and other wheres and cares
As he remains just "present" on an old blanket
With the serenity of azure sky
And a gentle breeze from over the countryside – then, a bit later,
After the picnic of unexpected delights, wine and song,
Relaxing, and sometimes dozing in idyll,
He simply watches the day change colors
As its denouement commences.
Still later, when the moon cries within its cloudy veils,
Whispering winds take up moaning round the eaves,
And the barren tree's attempt to sway
Has its gnarled branches
Scratch and tap a twiggy polyrhythm
On the rooftop and upper walls
And the clicking of raindrops becomes uncountable
He settles down for sleep … he knows … looks forward to
The morning … stepping outside,
Where there'll be pools reflecting the cool gray sky.
However, now
Inside – he recalls just how her tears brimmed
That once long ago, reflecting candle's light
And he, too, has a glimmer in his eye
As he snuffs out the candle at his bedside.

2) *Last night, the dream*

Through the window panes that reflect his face
He looks upon a dark, starless sky of rumpled black clouds.
He begins to suspect the slight sounds he hears
Are whispers.

The moon appeared but   only once
And vanished hopelessly
Beyond an eclipsing shroud of dark.
Finally, he turns from the window.

As he lay restless upon his bed,
Outside, in the hallway – he hears quick, light footsteps
As if someone was almost running back and forth
As if searching desperately for something valuable.

Then came a scratching at the door
Tentative, fearful
Hesitant, he went over
But keeping the chain on,
And staying well inside, he slyly opened for a peek.
No one could be seen.
After a minute, just as he was about to close the door –
He thought he heard a whisper
Curious, as he unchained the door and half stepped
A heavy chill draft poured down upon him
It was so like a current he looked up seeking its source
But saw only the ceiling
It was as if his feet were in a hard ice-cold keep
And then, when he stepped back,
This thick air was cloying, embracing him
And held on so

His hands went blue in doing so
He turned to face into his room
When there was a whisper
A warm breath … at his ear this time … he turned around
Expecting something, yes … but not
Her translucent presence
Standing but a hand's width away

Eye to eye with her ghostly face and blank stare
He looked on as she turned, walked out into the hall
When he looked out – after her
He saw her wisp of a form shivering
He recalled how such minor tremors
Would traverse her frame betimes
How, she might reach out then beseeching him
How her hand would tremble and be so frigid

But here, now?
He could hear her thin breath
See her cool white hand but ghostly
And when she turned to face him again
Did he imagine he could see it?
His dim reflection in her limpid eyes, which beheld him

He saw that, in her way, she beckoned to him
Without expression,
Imploring with the barest sidelong motion
Of her head

He could not doubt it was her spirit
The inviting curves, her braided hair, the burial smock
Then, of a sudden, and only in his mind, could he hear it,

That wailing, the kind only he would know,
From her final moments
Even as she appeared to be mute in expression
He knew that this would be broken with racking sobs
It was her
And sounds, echoing where none should,
Filled his mind –

He clasped his hands over his ears –
Useless, of course, as it ever was
The voiceless screams came through his thin defenses
He began his own incoherent babble of pain and remorse.
As if in reply, she wailed,
"Why, have you brought me here?"

"But," he stammered, in a hoarse whisper,
"What have I done?"

Her strength, never hardy, fails
Her ghostly form falls to the carpeted floor, in a heap,
And like a tenuous cloud dissolves into mist
Pouring down to pool over the floor
It flows toward him to collect at his feet
From this a pillar rises up before him – it is she – again
Barely erect – as if horribly aged and infirm
Her face contorts as if each movement is excruciating
Or such exertions are nearly beyond her meager allowance
Her wispy, quavering voice is incoherent – yet fervent.
He cannot make out the murmured phrase she repeats
Then, she begins casting frantic glances about as if
As if some noisome and horrible beast were nearby
And she's not sure in which direction to escape
She moves away ... looking this way and that

But as he motions toward her
She dissolves into a chaotic pool of light and shadow
And this etheric mass flows back toward him
And he steps back
Even as it vanishes before reaching his feet.

Shocked – he backs into his room, closes, then locks its door.
He fears to look about
The sole candle illuminating his dank chamber
Gives the flickering shadows monstrous airs
And when it gutters out
He sees a glowing mist transpiring through the door.
Transfixed he cannot help but watch
It reforms into the beauty he once knew.
She ignores him though
And looks about the room
As if to approve the accommodations
Her eyes catch sight of something
And without looking he knows
She has seen the framed picture of them,

She sensually walks to the table where it is set
Her illusory hands touch and then caressed it
In another moment
As if struck
She seems to buckle under   then ripple
With a cascade of invisible torments and blows

Unsteadily
She holds on to the table – needing its support
He sees her tears fall onto it
Iridescent pearls of vapor   they shatter and
Pool into a thin luminescent haze

It spreads over the table
A moment later, after reaching the edge,
There forms a threadlike waterfall,
Which vanishes into darkness before reaching the floor.
Then she stands
Cupping her hands at first to her breast as she faces him
He sees she has a gentle hold of something
Something that is moving, restive
Within her prayerful, peaceful hands
It seemed to him a shadowy shape
Something that shifts and seems slippery
He cannot look as she proffers it

But at the same time he cannot, for his life, avert his gaze
From the dark, ruddy, wet mass she holds out
As if in sympathy she whispers his name
Because of this
He is able to look into her clear blue eyes, instead,
Relieved to avoid looking upon what she bears him
All the while he understands her gaze is not on him
But on her gift   and he knows what it is
His eyes are drawn into hers
And he can't help but see what is reflected upon them
And in the reflection of each tear
As they race down her cheek and fall into vapor
Helplessly his sight is drawn along with their descent
Even as his horrified mind screams
He beholds that which she has cautiously kept to her breast

Despite his fears, his will,
And all the strength he might muster
His gaze fixates upon that which he would not see
In her angelic hands, cupped
He sees its muscular shrugs palpitating

How it is bruised and blue
And how, as her mystical tears fall upon it,
It begins to dissolve, horribly, into depending shreds
It's four chambers working to the very last
Each, as a mouth, babbling ...

In the morning
He knew that dreams walk this world
Just as surely as nightmares do
He knew that just as the waking world sleeps
So does the sleeping world wake
That only the mad know the difference
And no one listens to them or cares much
For what they say or do not say of what they know

In the morning   the brilliant sky
And the thin dusting of snow were terrifying
Their small portrait was still where she'd left it.

The pains began after breakfast
And the appointments not a week later
To the last of his days
He would remember the carnival ride where they met
Where and when he told her of his love
How she kissed him, tentatively ... first
And he could not help but regret the fall of their dreams
And the failings of his heart.

Tears

That the tune was forty years old
And I recalled shyly dancing when it was still gold
With a girl, long ago, cheek to cheek in the past
That's how old memories return, soft, sweet, and fast

I tuned to a story read live
While out for errands, an ordinary drive
For the song itself had brought tears to brim
So I was glad for something banal, even grim.

I listened on, in safety or so I thought
Until the woman mentioned her flight and they fought.
Between words, and quiet ones at that,
The couple fought with silence, as if it were a brickbat.

The two, vying to separate
When four white horses came by their house, very late.
Though she feared being bit, they were tame
And he tried acting kindly, but *it* was the same

When she stayed out petting them slowly
He knew she'd be leaving him, and coldly.
The finale and applause found me a wreck and rent.
And so I hardly heard its end, I was so spent.

Certainly those musicians had been adept
For what else could awaken what had so long slept?
And the story, fiction, mere words
So wherefore my tears when he saw migrating birds?

I sobbed through shuddering breath
While hot tears flowed and I thought of life and death
I couldn't see; I couldn't drive.
So I pulled into a lot to rest, or survive.

What was it about that old song?
What else on God's green earth could possibly go wrong?
Could a story bring this about?
Or could this be my kind of existential doubt?

I hunted up and down the dial
And regained my composure after a while
A blues tune came to the rescue
I loudly sang along heedless that I might be on view.

I couldn't care less, if anyone at all saw me there,
That the song clearly pegged me an aging old square,
For the hard storm had passed over
And, somehow, I managed this odd personality test

Midnight Hour

At night
When slight rain falls
Perhaps there is a tapping at the eaves
While on the windowpane
Moisture gathers up
Into further droplets
Which run down along irregular
Scribbled lines

Hours may pass
While even the most attentive of minds
When set to study such events
Will discern no pattern
No sense
And most would agree
That such intent forwards no real purpose
Why detail such records
As might be made
For they only appear to disappear
Again and again
As overlays compound
To completely cover up
What once was

Even the best of us
Might hope only
To recall – perhaps – take note
Of the rarities
A spectacular splash
How chance creates figures, a letter
The profile of a friend or eyes of a beast

Occasionally there is the silent illumination
Of distant lighting
This casts a fluctuating bluish light, which plays

And projects ghostly drops
Which then run and move
Upon other surfaces
A clocks face
This table's top or
The skin on the back of my hand

And when the light shifts – it moves those projections

In a display of stark relief

Moving my hand into the darkness
Avails nothing
For the mind has already seen the script of chaos
Upon its very flesh
And so the writ is all but secured in memoriam
Yes, you may forget it
But the flesh cannot
For the mind cannot
As for the heart
It will have taken in all that it can
Of those sublime connections
Not only between what is
And what is not
But between what has ever been
And will yet be!

S(o)me Advice At 40 …

Let my fingers type it,
If they know the way.

If my thoughts could see it,
They would certainly light this play!

Spring is in the butter –
Lambs are at suckle or bay,

Let me to the temperate fields –
With blossoms that buck in May

Falling leaves   twirl
Flicker in noon light   confuse
This butterflies path

Three

Passings and Life Notes

Puzzled Words Of Love

Always
forswear
slander,
wicked envy,
vehemence,
or to deceive –
nor let dire discontent torment
and tempt you.
Wherefore?
When you doth thus
sanctify your manner,
saying farewell
to poisonous melancholy's
mortal strike at one's bosom –
methinks myself we thus bestow love
unto our very dreams,
bringing too a merry grace,
light jest,
and measured mercy –
friend,
ne'er therefore yield
the fair breast,
vouchsafe it in full
lest death shalt thine only lover be.

I have yet to see Mom's grave, but I'll go; I know that much; her grave is next to Dad's. Odd that her middle name, Maria, was not given

Pinpricks, Needles, And Knives

Dropping a stitch,
Freeing a loop
From its hold,
Is nothing.
Nor, for that matter,
Is putting a word,
Or phrase,
Awry in a letter.
Such cute errata
May get their laughs,
But with repetition
Sobering thoughts
Are brought to bear.

Just as when birds go south,
The first few
Are never noticed –
As much as the flocks
Which overpass weeks later.

So, when hands miss,
Fail in their grip,
Or feet stumble themselves up
And there's nothing unusual
About forgetting –
There are those quiet,
Open moments,
When nothing seems as it is,
And the world, if this truly is one,
Appears only as you would have it –

And in time,
As seasons change the skies,
And cloud shadows slip over the hills,

By laying off work,
Setting projects aside,
And all the historical jetsam
Is to be cast off,
Left to shift in your turbulent wake.
You want to give everything away
But only if it is for the very best.

Rest assured, it will be.

For as certain as there are tracks
Leading through tall grasses
So there are those trails
Etched along the hillsides

Where, when remains are found,
They will provide, being rich in evident detail,
Substance for a moment of summation
Begging only for the closing of the tome.

51

Miss Nancy *(for Nancy Forest)*

I know you for your easily smiling face –
And your hands that help with unassuming grace.
You are the one who skips by with your class,
Your students trailing – all smiles as they pass.
You're the teacher, who brings the wild things inside,
So wide-eyed students learn how walking sticks abide.
When I visited your guitar class, each girl boasted loud;
Each wanted their turn to show off, so happy, so proud.

A proper teacher, however, you always kept your trim –
And are ever a gentle lady despite your humorous whim.
You are the hugger and caresser of each wounded soul.
Yours is the spirit keeping their moral compass whole.
For your children you make each day different and new;
Your way is to keep it fresh; they love learning, from you.
I say teaching is the most ancient of honored professions,
Which is to say – mothering – if you understand regressions.

Both are noble callings though each hardly gain their due –
But, excelling in both, we were fortunate to know you.
You taught with your heart; your students learned through play
And it's a rare teacher who succeeds in keeping to this way.
It's simple to say we're better for knowing you, Ms. Forest.
And harder to say we'll find one who does what you do best.
You know, love, like gold, is not where it may be found
Rather it is, as you make it, when generously passed around.

Know what might be called your living trust will endure:
All those petite souls, fostered by your love, simple and pure

From A Friend, For A Friend

There is time for everything,
However long you live,
If you think of everything
In terms of what you give.

In terms of what you give,
It is a balance act divined
Between having what you'd will
And when that must be declined.

And when that must be declined,
There is little left to say,
If love has kept unto your heart
While you give the self away.

While you give the self away,
Be trusting that love in turn
Will provide the bounty needed
From the lessons that you'll learn.

From the lessons that you'll learn,
You'll let no thing strike love's hold –
But bring sweet heaven into your breast
Where vouchsafed its bloom will unfold.

Jehanah hosted Sacred for over 20 years, was integral to it, and famed in her neighborhood and communities. She was known for being supportive of both poets and druids. I was privileged to hear her speak often and be a part of the huge crowd who heard her when she featured at the Koret Auditorium reading from her collected works: "Next Century's Child." We took her out to dinner for a great evening, but were shocked when she passed away two days later. She had a great, caring and loving voice!

Oh Jehannah!

She was a heart
She was a song
She was a poet
She was a beauty
She was a voice
She was a dancer
She was a lover
She was a mother
She was a sister
She was a voice
She was clear eyed and visionary
She was an elder with wisdom
She spoke of bears, forests, and stars
She was a voice
She was rock and stream
She was season and wind
She was fire and incense
She was cloud and illusion
She was a voice
She was a singer and teacher
She held the universe with care
She was kindly, soft seeming yet tempered
She spoke her mind, could laugh, and cry
She was a voice
She was a lover of learning, of leaving
She was a watcher of stars turn
She was mentoring, mild
She was Sacred Grounds
Where she'd let people hold time
And she was a voice full, honest, and loving,
Who helped others find theirs.

Crickets stop
        At my approach   begin again
      Behind me

This is Jim and I at a Sufi camp. The following poem "Three" was inspired by a graceful and grand meandering talk he, Bob, and I had at that Sufi camp. It was complete with philosophical asides, metaphysical ramifications, jokes, all of which, though so long ago now, were clear to me when I reviewed this poem.

Three

With old redwoods,
providing as much or more
patter as we.

On humble steps
My friends stood being well met,
aging friends three.

Speaking on life,
long tales, even of love –
older men, we.

Hardly mention
age, dreams, or the common woes –
our idyll free.

With tales, cock sure,
being butts of our own jokes,
laughing men we.

Soon the slow smiles,
and farewells in a grip, which
loving eyes see.

Later, amid
Oak and the Redwoods, singing
with my muse, I.

Walk with the cloud's
shadows passing on the road
Just ambling nigh.

To the circle
of dancers joining in the
audience, I.

Just toss it in,
a joke, as a shill as if
God might know why.

Drunk with the dance
faint with giving love's embrace
heart to heart I.

Pour forth the joy
serving one and all, as if
I had grace to ply.

Receipts In Account

In an apartment, on a shelf inside a blue felt bag
There is a rectangular wooden box.
It measures three, by eight, by twelve, cubic inches:
288 in all, an estate.

His place is nearly empty now.
Oh, there might be a couple of guitar picks,
Some ruined magazines, a shoestring, or a broken comb
Amid the dust, but really only oddments remain.

We'd broken apart his hand made fixtures:
Tables, bed, desk, and shelves.
And given away the kitchen spices to his teary neighbor.

We had the windows open to the cold
Even as we sneezed to the stirred up dust and mold.

A perfect San Francisco summer, windless,
A quiet gray sky oversaw our work.
We emptied his dwelling out.
Down came hangings, drapes and ad hoc window shades
Until nothing was left but holes in the walls
Or the brighter rectangles I recalled the pictures of.

Yet, I still found what I'd call a keepsake,
A knit cap, which he'd often worn, a good one,
While Bob chose an ancient cartoon off of the fridge.

Surprising, that some of the oddest little things,
Things no one wanted at the last garage sale,
Things no one thought to sell, or that found a price,
These, anonymous to anyone,
Brought up speculations
Forming a memorial, of sorts.

Bob had brought his horse trailer.
I helped him back it into the driveway
So we could toss things down from the upper windows.
After the apartment was left, ruinously vacant,
We went into the garage.

There, cardboard dreams were scattered on the floor
Also photos of a time when his vision became invention.
Here were his wishes of wrought metal,
Echoes of inspiration, the homespun gym,
Now nothing more than weights to be moved,
At long last, and for the last time.

Touching that worked metal,
Something as real as anything else in this world,
Where meaning is temporal, matter transient,
And all is transformed in the eyes of the beholder.

And there were the other remainders,
Items too precious or paltry to sell,
Arranged in stacks for the heirs apparent and not.
These were left by us,
Who were relieved and free to go.

Free – free to go?   when my own dreams
Became all the more dearly held
For what I've seen of those left by today?

This, another unexpected memorial, mutely testifying
To an inheritance,
Which brought me up short even as I received it.
Still, it was more than I'd expected.
And it was strange to feel so burdened
However empty handed I appeared to be.
A couple gross of cubic inches,
A half-century of life,

The assemblage of simple items
Awaiting their final dissemination,
And Good Will gains
What that garage sale didn't.
Then too, today, the day after, I wash out that knit cap.
Knowing that when I wear it, no matter how long from now,
I'll think of his laugh, how silly he could look,
And how little he cared about things just like that.

Gifts in giving, love in leaving, hope in grieving,
And something weightless in believing,
Timeless in receiving,
That which is both less than anything,
But far more than nothing at all.

Her phone call
She brings up the cancer
Letting me   off the hook

Solstice Night 2002

Solstice night

The wind combs over the beach

Coals

Skitter off and away

Across the glistening sand

Flying this way

And that

Flying and settling

Flying and winking   out

Embers rise on dark clouds

To a starlit sky

Confusing those heavenly lights

Magic

In the garden
behind the ruined old house
the plants have gone wild.
Stones in the pathway
have been overturned
by the avocado's roots.
Others lay buried
where the raised beds collapsed
until you'd hardly suspect
that there'd been any arrangement
of walkways at all.

Tall grasses and
wildflowers
in rank confusion;
the dropped plums and peaches
beneath their respective trees;
and swiss chard
has taken hold all along the tired fence.

I recognize
New Zealand spinach,
broken corn stalks,
and the new blackberry bramble.
I can tell
that the gardener
planted a variety of squash
and tomatoes.
It looks as though
this garden was left,
abandoned really,
in a heartbeat
by whoever lived here.

I must get back
to our wild picnic.
Like everyone else, I too
had been sent out to find
food to bring back,
our little tradition.

I did not think
I'd find anything
over that dry grassy hill
but that
was the unpromising lot I drew.

This place, though,
appeared
so unexpectedly
as I thrashed through underbrush
trying to find anything at all.

At first I did not know
I'd found the ivy-covered wall of the house
leaning out toward me
as I drew aside a branch.

The rank garden is a trove!
I will be the one
who brings just desserts,
as if by magic:
sweet plums and peaches,
luscious avocados,
several huge sun ripe tomatoes,
and enough greens
to make everyone groan!

Once Upon San Francisco
With regards to S.P. Mackin

A light fog   graces San Francisco's Sunset
Just outside Café Flore … and … looking toward the ocean
All is fog shrouded – just six short blocks hence
Parnassus, likewise, remains occluded
And there is quiet – a hush
As if the whole of the world
And all upon it
Were whispering only … and the sun taking it easy

Colorful fallen leaves decorate the sidewalk
As the N Judah glides along … with grace
Absent its usual clatter and squeals

A young crowd is inside
Their ambient chatter speaks of ease
On a weekend's concluding portion
The only exceptions
To this mulled settling
Are the espresso machine's hiss
And Jerry Garcias' eclectic, meandering solo
Over the PA

A pedestrian couple stops
Idles look in at each other then enters
Peter greets them – smiling, conversational – without haste
His hands held in front sometimes working his red apron

I am, for once, at ease myself, having splurged on treats
First a big, deep, hearty mug of coffee
Then the ciabatta – housing caramelized onion
Topped with melted jalapeno jack,
Raw spinach, avocado, thickly sliced tomatoes
And a creamy, dreamy dressing

Slowly … I … let each bite … dissolve
Next time – I'll try the Genoa!
The skylight informs me of the weather
When there's a brightening
The ceiling fan's shadow
Circles near my feet and time, that unenviable creature,
Makes its own marks –
Charting its inevitable passage toward the future

I give my regards to Peter who waves me on
Board the N Judah and go down to Ocean Beach

I stroll pathways through dune grass … find a proper niche
And settle down there in comfort
Sunset colored waters swirl
As they overlap the glistening sands
A bright tumult tops those waves farther out
And the blue gray calm Pacific beyond is a wonder
I people watch for a time

Soon then … closing my eyes
I take in salty air
Hear waves swell and rush and sound
As my own breathing goes along and I reflect
Upon everything that comes to mind
Dissolve each thought as it arises
Over and over and over

Until … in a unique silence … I'm free
Of all those thoughts which disguise themselves as me
With no sense of time – no reason, no rhyme
And nothing further to inquire … nothing at all to desire
And I sense, in the ebb and flow of my breathing
That I too … transpire!

Thanksgiving Haiku
(A linked set of Haiku)

His new liver in,
the rock star very cheerful
on this Thanksgiving

The red gore glistens –
the torn rat and flies –
among redwoods this morning

Among the redwoods –
hardly a bird or sound
I begin to sing.

crowded – gorging the grate
dead leaves gathered
at the confluence of the corner

full moon in fall
the wind sounds around the corner
high clouds move   still stars

on her walk   the car
alarm goes   motion sensor
lights   her moon face

Solstice 2003

On the narrow strand,
With the darkened ocean at our backs
The vast continent lay before us
Already fallen into darkling tracts

From here we saw the sovereign's descent
And kept the solstice watch as the pyre was spent

Only one other flame a half-mile north flickered spare
Where a blackout silhouetted the hills beyond it there

We few, stood beneath a beclouded moonless sky
Huddled as swirling mists occluded the passers by

Firm eucalyptus and birch burned well enough
Atop the oaken coals, our fire was hot and tough

At our position, it couldn't be called a beachhead,
We held forth in music and song as the tide retreated

I stood at the edge of the foam looked back to my friends
Imagining our land stretched thin and grasping for its ends

How now? That in darkness profound,
We've naught but our lovely Christmas days
While ahead portends a new year's war
Despite the ministering and public displays.

Four

On Poetry, Art, and Perceptions

Upon Being Asked: "Who Influenced You?"

How and when does a story begin? How are we to know?
When I think on it, any tale
No matter its size, must begin long ago.
So when asked who influenced me
I gave my friend an analogy.
Consider a stream, I said, even a small one, near to hand
Is not its course ever guided by contours of the land?
Is it not deflected by every rock, bit of soil or living thing
With which it co-exists
Before or after the stony lip of its spring?
And are not all these things but a postscript
Proceeding from a source,
Which charges the nature of the stream,
And so effects its discourse?
Nor should I fail to say that forests and men
Alike surely do amend it
For its worth is clear to those temporal beings
Who can apprehend it.
But the fishes and all the living things cannot be the stream,
Nor, for that matter, can it be the water, or so it would seem
For the flow is ever carried off, even as we watch, for sport
Whether by evaporation or gravity's simple transport.
It is surely not its path, or the things it has carried off,
Nor could it be its remains, a shallow drying trough.
A stream then is a time and place, dependent on conditions
Which, truth be told, have utmost antiquity as its origins,
Preconditions, which, if scientifically analyzed, with-all
Stretch back to the beginnings of time immemorial
And, perforce, do they not, I waxed, extend onward in time
Until the edge of doom itself, imagine a stream – so sublime!
And so full circle I came as my analogy found its end.
What are the credits I must roll to answer my friend?
No less than everyone who has ever been or may yet be
Not less than the full chorus, say I, clearly influenced me.

Light, Light, Light

From the start of this universe   until now
There has always been the light
Clearly it is an essential factor
For what else do we all come to eventually and a'right
But the light, light, light?
No thing overshadows this
It's what moves this poor body
Causes my fingers to trace such moments as this
Councils the passion coursing my heart well
And what so enlivens my giddy soul tonight
But the light, light, light?

Terms cannot describe or contain this
Actions provide mere indications
Lyrics might bear it so long as breath bears them
Nothing temporal can truly be seen without it
And all things eternal are made up only of it
What else moves us within so as to create without
Passing for inspiration's sight
But the light, light, light?

And so in the deep, cold world of winter
When sullen, lifeless, and leaden heavens
Occlude the hope of celestial bodies
When the landscape beneath
Is set in a monochromatic display
Yes, fish may still seize the day beneath their ice,
Yes, furtive, burrowing survivors do abide,
And the heart of an owl harbors its heated blood,
As it wings down silently after sighting its prey
Dark talons clutch the unwary or luckless
Where blood spatters on moonlit white
What else rules there
But the light, light, light?

What muffles the tolling bell better
Than distance and time?
What rings it ever clearer to echo in the mind?
What's the message it means to send
All these years later?

What do I do by telling you this?
Why do such words as these make their way here?
What causes my spirit to soar
My heart then mind to quicken?

What makes a singular difference
No matter how seemingly slight
But the light, light, light?

When death is no longer that distant, dismissed threat
But present, promised and immediately certain
Your intimate companion, if you will
Waiting on you, so to speak, hand and foot
What will move still   until that very last?
What makes its essential difference felt?
What else is there   to keep in sight?
But the light, light, light?

Long After Time   What Is?

Long, long from now
When all that is now   is forgotten
More than simply buried in the mind
Or the earth
More than simply covered up
But gone
Truly dissolved through the immense passages of time
During which the Earth has completely reformed its surface
And is done turning under its continents
When every human thing has vanished
Beyond all hope of ever being found
When no living thing recalls our peculiar smell or fear
And life has recovered all that was lost.

When all that is now
Is absolutely gone
Beyond anyone's knowledge of what once was
Is   or might yet be –

Long after time
When there is no forgiving
Or forgetting
When the quiet world simply rests
Through its long horizons
And the moon casts down innocent light
Where winds are gentle
And the forests have come back into their own
Long after
Long, long after all that we've dreamt of
When even the greatest of our myriad possessions
Have been broken down into the smallest of grains
And so have become part and parcel to the earth
And each is simply moved by the wind   or the water
And all has been absorbed by

And recycled millions of times
Through plants and animals
The living carpet that life is upon this world
When there is no evidence of any kind
When matter is so purified
Until purity is no longer a relative term
And all is well.

Long after time has gone
When it is no longer a measure
When measuring is no longer needful
When counting is as forgotten as numbers
And sense is a term applied
Only to the eyes, ears, tongue, nose, or touch.

Long after time what is?

What will be?

When peace itself is the only thing
And nature is let to do what it does best
After the recycling of all that we once were
Has erased all the details
Leveled the playing field
Once and for all

Long after
Long, long after time
What is the chance
That the Earth will decide to try once more
To weave spirit into matter
Manifesting such illumination
As brings consciousness into life
And if not in human form…
Then certainly with a prayer that this time
Its promise will be kept!

This is at Sacred Grounds soon after I began hosting that venue.

Under these leaves
All of the haiku   millions
And millions of millions

Sidewalk puddle
Snowflakes   and their reflections
Vanish together

Seekers Need Not Apply

It's said poets are inspired by the quintessence of beauty
That they purpose their lives
Around a quest for that theoretical bauble
And I understand – for that effort is paramount in my life –
Which is why I can describe myself as … a poet
But when a woman-friend inquired … wanting to
"know more about magical text"
I suspected *someone* yearned to be a poet
So I began my dissuasions,
"Ye Gods!" as my Mom would say,
"Don't be precipitous; listen!"

"When I hear people bemoan their circumstances
Lacks, wants, or whatever, I sometimes laugh out-loud
Then, apologize to make amends, if I can.
You see, sometimes I can't explain myself quickly enough
And so have destroyed dates or fouled up friendships
But, if they do listen, this is what I tell them:
At least THEIR kind of problem CAN be solved,
They CAN find a job or change careers … find another lover,
CAN ignore problems until time just sweeps them away,
CAN just pack up and leave a marriage, a job, whatever,
And, if all else fails,
CAN just lose themselves … in drink, drugs
Or, if romantic at heart, play with suicide."

"Poets aren't so lucky," I told her.
"We NEVER find the ends to our means
After all, how likely is it that that great wonder
The Inspiration,
Will result in a gloriously eternal 'meisterstuck'
My " 'be all and end all?' "
Then, looking her straight in the eyes, I added:
"While it can't be zero, there's no term small enough

For an event that's never happened, but might yet still
Poets are, in this additional sense, worse off than anyone."
"And now for the bad news,
Poetry is an individual's affair with the muse
And so it's a journey that will not quit them.
I can no sooner leave off musing than I can leave off being!
I am as bound to it as I am to my soul.
And poets, being their own boss, judge, jury, and executioner,
Hear no pleading, allow no escapes,
Nor is there mercy to be had for the asking."

"And this doesn't change with time or success –
Such as the latter term might apply to poets –
Or due to their all to common failings
Which can't be beat – either in their variety or largesse."

"It doesn't change with talent or ignominiousness either
After all, who, besides poets, listen –
Much less understand
Just exactly what it is poets do do
Or what the bleeping double H ell they're talking about
All while, again and again, amazingly, they proceed on
No matter gravity or consequence"

"The only good news comes in the form of a lack
Poets needn't worry about managing 'their business.'
Since there isn't any, practically speaking, to speak of"

I paused to let that sink in, "Which gets us back to why
Why a 'salt of the earth' person, such as you," I told her,
"Would want to be 'liberated' as you believe I am.
What could the attraction be in your eyes?
What benefits do you imagine flow?
What do you think you'll get
By exchanging that 'so called' ephemeral gain
For a raft of temporal and existential pain?"

So she said, "But, my dear, love certainly has its mysteries."
"Well, " I said, "to that I owe."
I mean what else could I say?
"Still," I added, "I'll not advise taking up 'the word'
I've made my choice and taken my chance
It's gotten so I can't tell which is which anymore
But my dear ... my darling
I fear my dissuasions will fail and you'll persist!
So you must be warned – there'll be no end of it
Make sure you know that – because there is no end
To the soul's musical presentations
So long as you live and breathe!"

"Oh, but wait, as they say, that's not all
There's much, much more ...
You could wind up in books
Read hundreds of years from now
Be the subject of intense speculation from academics who,
For God's sake, are friggin' clueless or, worse yet,
Very dry of wit – English say –
And so painfully arrogant.
Imagine that sort of animal
Propounding upon you, their tortured subject
Whose scribbled remains must testify on their own behalf
And who must suffer a series of dissertational dissections –
Imagine such a dull and shallow pan
Attempting to sift what is, essentially, God's bright gold?"

"Yes – they may know your biography
That you, for example, traced a figure upon a frosty pane,
Which disappeared with your breath centuries ago
But not what the figure was ... meant
Nor what was reflected in that hazy pane
Or seen through the liquid clarity
Of script upon night's glass?
Not to mention how you saw through what you saw

To begin yet another communion
With the infinite and eternal –
Ultimately they'll ignore that element
For its consideration beguiles even the best of us
And will obfuscate
Before obstructing all their considerations.
Truth be told, the best they might get is a sorry sally
Into the soundless mist of incomplete dreams … while,
Those of them more clever,
May reach for what they imagine imagination to be
In the hopes of extracting from the heavenly realms
Something of your attraction to it.
But they will have no idea, my dear, of who you are
For all their efforts
You will be beyond them, their traceries or descriptions
And be as much a puzzle to them
As you are, right now, to yourself … for all that
Imagine that … for all that … you will ever be a mystery."

"And so they'll make mistakes which will live on and on
While you, in turn, turn helplessly in your grave"

"So – I've said enough – fly, if you will, into the airy realm
But know fate will be the wind beneath your wings
Take heart in nothing less than the all-encompassing universe
Because, if the inspiration of the muse is what you want,
You're sure to have your way
Just as she'll have hers with you
So, my dear, just be sure you want it
And its entire, unshakeable entourage – no matter time, space
Or any other dimension you care to list.
Make sure you know eternity may well be yours."

Here I am presenting poetry at The Cultural Integration Fellowship, a wonderful place. This is most likely during one of Sally Love Saunders' events.

As he begins
To strike his Tibetan drum
Quiet distant lightning

Above the garden
With mountains and plains beyond
White butterflies entwine

The Manifold Manners Of Means:

Through a flower's flow of colors
And autumn wind's undone
And the still white of the winter
Under a sharp and glinting sun;

Through a meal with good old friends
All with family heartily bound
And the stories by the campfire
And songs that are pass'd 'round;

Through the smells of summer grasses,
Through the Redwood dells a' dawn,
After moonless nights, a' sunrise,
Where to gleaming shores we've gone;

Through the words we banter daily,
The common office jest,
Through the phrases that we know by,
That language we speak best;

Through the hearts on fire – and winging,
Through the thoughts that wing o'er the swell,
Through the spirit that comes unto us,
We know we're one as well.

The community of the heart brings one
On tender, on above
To present the present to us
In the quietest ways of love

The quietest way,
 The quietest ways,
    In the quietest way
        Of love:

With each breath we breathe
In each moment that we last,
Before our eyes, in an eye's blink,
We make the future and the past!

And so it happens that each day,
Whether by chance or through an old song,
Opportunity will knock as you go –
To pass life's tune along.

Ocean Beach, Remnants

The night's beach, breeze blown in from afar,
Above the sound I pick out one star.
The rim of foam at the edge of a wave
Sweeps over sand, I recall his grave.
After New Years, when he was turned in,
I tossed the red clay to rebound on his coffin.
I stood and spoke to the handful there.
Not knowing them though my words were spare.

We did break bread, jammed, and what's more:
We'd muse upon life and so shared our store.
Five at his grave saw his mother weep.
Her empty hands had nothing to keep.
"But what will suffice," I'd asked him one night,
"For life to seem that you've lived it aright?"
A cynic he, staring beyond the sea wall,
Said, "Why, by life's end you'll have nothing at all!"

"Life conspires," he said, "going wither it may,
So one can't hope to plan, not even a day –
Each year brings chaos and blind decades come fast –
Nothing's of use, for time's sure scythe takes all that would last."
Bitter words they, but now what would I see?
What would I choose for my own legacy?
Cutting myself to the quick, I did recollect this:
My dear sleepy wife and this morning's kiss.

Our rollicking laughter and her little half smile,
How she's graceful in dance and my love all the while.
It's Love, I should've said to him, which, if passed around,
Provides all posterity with subtle gifts profound.

Ode To Pee

Bless this water
That has passed through me
Bless this water on its way
To the wine dark sea
May this water
Catch a moonbeam's glint just so
To shimmer in the eyes
Of a beauty's ardent face aglow
Bless it and all the waters
With which it flows and blends
Bless that and all the air
In which its mingling vapor ascends
By this means bless the seven winds
Which carry it away and over the seven seas
To mountains, farmlands – every hill and dale
And into coastal fogs where it precipitates from trees
Nor forget sunset – where its gleaming prism catches
The sovereign's blazing rainbow hues or,
In the moon's silvery light,
Plays it at the limb of our pellicle of atmosphere
To cast an eerie halo of high austere icy delight
Bless this water
That once was I
That once was a part
Of my heart's mind and (eye)
Bless this water
From the one cup we share
Bless the passing
Of excess to spare
Yes, blessings pour – each drop from the sky
To clothe the world in the greenery we espy
Forever a river flows through us, within
Thus do I offer unto thee
My singular ode to pee

The Provisional Toast

Just because I have taken pause to wonder out loud, lad,
As to where we're bounden on this our uncertain sea.
You say, "Ah, my lad, here's not only to thee and to me
But to all of those creatures with souls who might come to be"

"In expansion," you go on, "let's raise flagons to those on high
And pray that our calling thus will bring angelic spirits nigh
For we're agreed that we may not find any sweet harbor,
Its welcome rest, or feast, or jest beneath a blooming arbor."

"And we know it matters not we recall sweet freedom's air
When we're companioned with the myth of your dark despair.
Yet dissent, each from the other, as to heaven's view?
On our burdens, which admix the saintly and earthly too?"

I reply, "Yes, but in our hearts, we both keep the holy realm
And pray, in our way, for God to take a hand at our little helm
And that through our faith will he captain us
Though the wheel be in our hands,
To a warm, soft shallow sea
Where we'll beach to berth on dreamy golden sands."

Blue under blue haze
Lake Tahoe in the distance
From the windy pass

1

birth

clothes

death

2

birth

clothes
death
clothes

birth

3

birth

clothes

death
clothes
birth

clothes

death

Hope

The house was empty
I was eating cold beans, rice with salsa, and an avocado
It hadn't been the best of days
There were troubles at work
I had some of my own
And those of the world overshadowed these
So I tuned in the airwaves
In the blink of an eye a Goddess of the air
Was asking, "What are you grateful for? Let me know."

I was struck   the very idea   what WAS I grateful for?
Stirred and disturbed
A rising maelstrom of unease
Caught at my breath   I stilled   braced
The upwelling force of heat
My heart strained
And eyes brimmed   over filled
And those precious jewels poured forth

My silent reply to her was for hope   hope
Was what I was thankful for this Christmas season
Without cause, pause or reason
A simple joy of the breast
Which soothes and warms
As does a Yule log glowing in its hearth
Mantled as it is
And, mantled as I am,
I harbor hope   with so little reason
In fact with none at all
Hope   the still peace of which the soul sings
In strains so sweet
Hope   flying in the face of hard-nosed facts
Or the perceptions of the mind's simple eye
And it doesn't matter if it's only you or I

Who harbor this delicious source
Even were that so
It would be all the more worthy a treasure
Such a rare gift of heaven's breadth
It illuminates the transcendent cause or rule
And hope is as faith is, "the substance of things
Hoped for, the evidence of things not seen …
Faith is the bird that sings while dawn is still dark"*

And it's what I was thankful for
Even though it seemed of no use
When there was no apparent path
No solution, answer or resolution
When nothing provided surcease of my heartache
Hope   needs no evidence   it is the evidence
Hope needs no cause   it is cause enough
Hope can provide where nothing else will
For it needs nothing, is nothing and takes nothing
Even as it gives of itself … away

It's as timely as your next wish
No farther away than your next breath
And, intimate as each and every heartbeat must be
Hope, dear friends
Hope is what I was grateful for
And that's what I would have told her
If I could have gotten through on that lone, low, wintry day.

*Often attributed to Rabindranath Tagore

Five

More Politics as Unusual

Fair Helen

Aeolian stars, soft night air,
Aegean beauty ever fair
Dancing through the hall in her prime
Sweet Helen loses no grace with time.
Millennium's girl, it is true,
I still fashion a blush on you.
Your sweet glances caught, shimmering
While lyre and muse set singing.
Ardent whispers given and caught
While no one knew what would be wrought.
Sweet Helen's constellate beauty
Was their clarion for duty.
They set sail for Ilium bound
And brought its battlements to ground;
Fervent love returned at last
Forgiven all for what was past.

And when, in time, your guise gave way
The vigil was kept night and day.
Men stayed on, stood close at hand
Guarding the treasure of their land.
Then, when your blink was slowly missed,
A maiden's hand touched at your wrist.
But here, now, though ages have passed,
Your beauty continues to last.
What is the mystery we have here?
Why should this tale be so dear?
Could it simply somehow be
A story worth eternity?
Or do we now lack their sense?
Docs it chide our indifference?
Dear sweet Helen I give you this,
My respect, in a lover's kiss.

Being Of Use

Leaves fallen to ground
By the thousands of millions
All over the fields
Of what was once
Honorable, strong, summer green.

Above, the simple cerulean
Stares at nothing
And everything in particular.
You and I, who know better,
Say nothing or what's less:
Bothering ourselves with dissections of the ordinary
Picking apart careers, decisions,
Our woeful affairs and aging lots.

We may hope for better times;
We may believe
That it's all just SNAFU;
Nothing to write home about.
But the leaves continue to fall
Unseasonably, without reason
And there is less and less cover
For the truth of the matter
To remain hidden by.

We begin to see the forest for the trees.
The ghosts of our forefathers whisper
Where the wind once rustled.
The roots are endangered;
The branches die out –
And their handiwork rots away:
The tarnish on the scales and sword,
Their sacred trust – violated
Our inheritance squandered.

So that now what was once so worthy,
So deserving of their spilt blood
And sacrifice,
Is despoiled, wantonly disregarded
Seen as encumbering, inconvenient.
As for "the people"
They are viewed as targets
Best left for juniors' sound bites,
Or stumping sermons.

Being neither falcon nor falconer.
I, for one, am lost without our center,
Yet I would stay on,
Yielding not, to the sway –

He casts occlusion both far and wide
Upon the light our illumined founders' eyed,
Let not this fell pretender's hand of slight
Obscure our elder's guiding light!

Yet, inquiring minds hardly want to know
Instead, there is the cathode's cold blue
Flickering behind each and every (pane).
While outside, in the chill night,
Beneath the naked stars and dark,
Silent as still air, and gesturing his mark,
A cowled and familiar shade passes them all by.
Mark you the deep-set eyes of a ruddy glow
The movements which seem to slip and flow
As if he were only a full moon's shadow.

To no avail will they be, their prayers made,
Or imprecations, when all petitions are stayed.
For His dark wind will sweep all those leaves away
Portending the gale, which the unpaid piper will play.

The Archer

1

Not quite instantly
Does thought, the will to power,
Charge currents
Through neuron circuits
To direct the broad of the back
Sweep up the arms
Command the hands
And fingers
All implements of duty
As it has the eyes fix
And focus.

When drawing the bow
To its set point
One aims
Eyeing in
As the breath is paused
Held at bay until –
With its gradual release
The sight is brought down
And slowly drawn to the target

The decision to loose an arrow
Is as much a choice
As it is a hope
And
When
Loosed
The fletching flutters
And the shaft's line
Is always true to its mark
If not yours

2

Far, far in the north
Still waters run the deeps
The ocean's conveyance is dispensed with   as is its salary
Thus time and the ice both grow thin

Thawing
The icy grip relaxes
And the remaining reserve
That breadth
Between running out and letting go

Closes

Salud, I say, L'chaim!

While we're here, now
We may as well enjoy this intermission
The marvelous interlude

The calm
Before Mother Earth
Pulls   drawing back all the forces
At her disposal
Arching across the horizon

To her set point

As she takes aim
Though not only at us
Rather at her real target
Which we just happen to obscure

Headlines And Frontlines

Who is on station, keeping watch?
Where are the frontlines?
We can see the small circles colored in
On maps of Turkey and the "Stans"
Or the rash overspread in Iraq,
These are the usual suspects
Commonly held as frontlines

But, on the Golden Gate,
A camouflaged vehicle is parked –
At ease nearby
Two soldiers, weapons slung on their shoulders.
Looking at their non-issue wraparounds,
Their eyes are hidden from view,
The sun's glinting gleam slips along silver rims
Edging my awareness
And I see their presence
As a newer, kinder, gentler, frontier, frontline

Long and torturous then
The frontline runs through every place,
Tangled and spaghettied,
Crossing the wires, bringing us news.
It's in the news speak
Punctuating the fabric of our lives
Point by needled point.
Insinuations whip-stitched to penetrate the warp and woof,
Of our day to day world
Along these lines we are strung out
With the lies that affront:
The airport's blinkless computers,
The digital doppelgangers ranked and filed by the millions,
And blinkered thinking hemming Constitutional exercise

It is the loopholes made to twist
Into knots, pressing into the skin,
As they tighten about the wrists
It is the whorls in signatures on unseen warrants,
The lines someone signs on,
Or the perimeter of Camp X-Ray.

As frontlines become headlines
Headlines become the frontlines
In the fourth estate
Fifth columns advance across the dailies
Yellowing the journalism,
Cut off, surrounded, hold-out Op-Ed's are co-opted
As slowly, surely, each word, every line, affronts.

Reading, I can't help but observe
The shifting lies we are given to believe
In this general retreat
I fall back, sniping, sorting out fictions
Inevitably creating yet another frontline
Drawn between that which I can and cannot accept.
Then too, the frontline is here, before my eyes
It is crossing of the "T" that wouldn't otherwise be written,
Perforce, it's my body's silhouette when I take to the streets
The sound waves of my voice as I rage at a solstice fire.

Telling jokes that ridicule, also affront

Or a synapse firing across that miniscule gap
The trace of chemical reactions
That arc between dendrites
If the thought would be suspect
We're asked to look out for the stranger,
Reports suspicions,
So, now, a second glance, a raised brow are frontlines
Which, increasingly, are in the eyes of the beholder

And when someone asks
What I'd say to those who wage this war
I find the frontline
Is at the heart of what is the matter,

I can't recuse myself from the disheartening disconnect
Between the high purpose this nation was born to
And the state to which we've fallen

When we are asked not to question,
Believe fraudulent, incompetent leaders,
And ignore how these few, have done so damned much
To so very many in so brief a time –
That it simply beggars the imagination –
Such a question becomes a burden
Unexpectedly heavy and drear
But then, there is nothing for it,
If I choose to live –
Because with each painful beat
I am reminded that my heart
Has been run through
And it is on the line –
So I'll have no solace
For I cannot back away,
Or turn about face,
Because there'd be no real time
Between that kind of choice
And a living death.

Coring them out
Purple sprouts   from red potatoes
Afghanistan's news

Protest!
  Doesn't get any footage
    At the Superbowl   see BS

Gaza   dynamite
      At their hearts   splattering
      Thoughts   and   arguments

Bush:
  Unadulterated asshole
    Or not … that's the question

Hot still   July
Listless teacher's conference   outside
For all to hear   ardent doves coo!

Pilgrim!

There are plains and seas.
The caged cannot touch them.
In prison, horizons are intimate.
Where, only two steps beyond the bar,
Lay a region as remote as Himalayan wilds
For all that   when so fixed,
One comes to understand
The intimate nature of the private universe –
Where your will still is possessed of choice,
In the midway
Between the zenith and nadir of the dreamlands –

Where, despite conundrums in the scales of injustice,
It is the fantasy of wall and bar, which you behold, and
Your outstretching, out-sourcing soul embodies this truth:
There are ever more spacious perspectives,
Limitless, in fact, and the soul's flight,
May swoop toward the boundless immensities,
Plunging dizzily over horizon's end over end
Delving until, beyond the point of collapse,
You cannot further.
And in that cloak of time and space
The fulcrum of your soul
Is meet with the axis upon which the universe itself turns
And there, so held (rapt) with beholding the Truth,
The Muse, the (aery) light, which thereat plays
Is this locus, which cannot be shut in or out,
Which is beyond all things and,
Just as your perfect being is,
Cannot be touched or denied – indeed – for it is everywhere,
And you, wherever you be, are a pilgrim
So, (bare) your (feet)
(F(o)r) the place yo(u) stand   is holy ground!

Lunch Time Bell

It was lunchtime
After a morning of meetings and conferences
Made pleasant by a sprinkling of small talk
Thankfully found in the nooks and crannies
Unintended by the event's planners

At lunch the old high school's cafeteria was full
People chatted at small tables
So the room had a gentle ambience
Of friendly murmuring

My back to the wall of
Windows open to the empty playground
The sunlight warmed my shoulders and back

The man I was talking to was pleasant enough
And our topics casual, as if in idyll really
As segues or associations
Both random and purposeful were made

At noon, I would guess,
The air raid siren went off
Both of us gave pause … mid phase
And looked each other in the eye
When I looked around
All I saw were people at table, laughing … relaxed
And this tall guy stretching out his legs

When I looked back to my companion
He was giving me a bemused sort of look
And said "duck and cover?"

I laughed as I got it
He was my age

He'd recalled the real deal
The cold war's hot nightmare
The one we used to see on TV
In movies or in safety films
I didn't have to say much
About those duck and cover drills

We laughed again because neither of us knew
Where the nearest air raid shelter was
Or what A-Bomb procedures would be now-a-days

But that was all there was to it or so I thought
And we let our conversation wander again
It was just an ordinary day
And the siren had blared on unnoticed
I thought an age that shouldn't have been forgotten –
Had been

Looking about as I listened to him
I wondered if they, being ignorant of history,
Would bear its repetition
I wondered how many heard it for what it was

How many of them, in their mind's eye
Saw those grainy black and white films
Where, in darkness, a bleak horizon
Is shattered by a brilliance
Which then curdles up
Into a towering mushroom cloud –
Or the one showing a pilot's long view down
Far above a scattering of low clouds
Where upon a calm blue green sea
A flotilla is set out
Then a flash at dead center whites out the screen
Clears in blink to let you see a circular shockwave
Rapidly encompassing the fleet

Or that model town
With store dummies in frame houses
In parked cars along mock streets
Being blasted by a sudden horrifically violent, dusty wind
And who can forget Strangelove's dark humor
The post-apocalyptic literature of the anti-hero
As well as the never-ending train of films
Starting with Godzilla
And all the other radioactive monsters or aliens
Who destroyed a world – which looked just like our own
Except for one thing,
And that difference was as simple as it is important,
In all those films the people found their way
To the truth, justice
And an all American happy-ending

Handwritten sign
On the red Ferrari for sale
Illegible details

In the Tenderloin
Flapping along in chill winter breeze
Pink Valentine's heart

NAZI Amerika *(2008)*

*In the tumult of G.W., the global village idiot, Bush, I
constructed explanatory theories such as this. Couldn't a group
with vast wealth, dedication, motive, and means and with its
scientists and intelligence operatives in the United States, Great
Britain, and Soviet Russia, on both sides of the Cold War, still
soldier on? Are "they" still players and we, of the western
world, being played?*

We can hardly wait for our turn, in 2008
I have to say for that for us, it will be great!
With love being the whole of our law too
Yes, love under will has our force made whole and new
It is we who direct the ships of state for our will yet endures
Through those who front our purposes as being wholly yours.
We shift the fronts of storm clouds, craft the news good and ill
And it's we who are the directors, doctors all with rare skill.

We didn't need an "October Surprise" to elect that stupid man.
We had the time needed to run him through our plan
Why, it seems now to have been the easiest of operations
So successful it's as if we planned to divest of the Germans
So rest assured, my friend, you can be sure
That that's exactly what we've planned, to give you our cure
So that your eternal rest will be our gift, your lot
And so, I say to Amerika, you are the fools – are you not?

You thought you could cut us a deal, offering us table scraps
At the end of our most recent war it was your silly mental lapse
To not realize at all, that, for us, it was the start of another go
One more beginning of many in the long way that we know
And, depending on which of us you may happen ask,
We've been centuries, even millennia at our long task
And our single most failure was not seeing the obvious value
Of the "new worlds" discovery, a mistake we came to rue

But even as you began your slow climb to the stars
So were we planting our own amid your founding fathers
Yes, just as with the Russians who had had their hey day
Now, we reap good profits as we guide your geopolitical play
The math was moronic and simple: as we taught
We, playing both ends for middle, won, as you both fought
And when "your" atom secrets somehow went astray

No one laughed any harder than us that rainy December day,
Which was doubly rich with the deep and subtle irony,
Having a Jew take the fall? Why we laughed with glee!
How precious was that smearing of an already besmirched race
The Rosenbergs were just the first we then picked up the pace
Yes, we're quite happy that all the Jews are in one place
Fighting each and every day for the sake of their holy place
Don't you think it clever of us? Don't you find it ironic?
For us we find it refreshing, a bracer if you will, quite a tonic

And of course you don't know of our inspired plan
That we'd get you to give them get their homeland
To simply put them all, for once, in their place
Mash for the pigs, as my folks used to say, of kitchen waste
And don't we just celebrate at your and their expense
Keeping them so dependant on the West for their defense
We've them to thank for the our hidden hold on Palestine
They stand in our stead in that bloody queue, how divine.

This brings to mind old Senator McCarthy and his scare
Who would turn over in his grave if we gave him his share
As would MacArthur, Truman, or Eisenhower, for that matter
If they'd had any idea – how we served them up, on a platter!
But as managers we salute each marvelous player
Praise them as we did Johnson or Regan the Evil Empire slayer
And though it was shame about Kennedy, he took that fall
Who thought he'd ever be elected, a Catholic, after all.

And the policy of containment, simply wonderful for us, no?
Putting our fingers into every pie there was, isn't that so?
A true world-girdling alliance; we clearly recommended it
And Amerika took our bait, played the game, the whole bit
And didn't we drink to you, Amerika of the fifties
Colossal fool that you were being directed with ease
To stumble, or so it would seem and for what it's worth
Into all the messy, darkling killing fields of this earth.

We knew the "Iron Curtain" and, if you'll pardon the analogy.
We were the playwrights and performed it as a tragedy.
We made its props, curtain calls, and gave stage directions
Hired the ushers, ticket takers, stage hands, and public relations
Remember we knew both sides of that set up, believe me
Next time you talk over what you call the cold war's history
Or recount its struggles or debate the counting of coup –
Imagine our nods, smirks or "high fives" if you will, as you do

Our connections are clear: we worked both sides' intelligence
Which then informed the policy of many a country, hence
Most all heed or hearken to our quite well-trusted word
Taking it at face value so now all have to do is ride herd
And you move men and mountains of machinery at our behest
Take the struggle we bequeath: preeminence for the West
The Jews in sufferance, modeling peace, work for us
And the well as America's camouflaged bungling, or chaos

Now this least best administration, profitable, as indexes show,
Bush puppeteers pull his strings to *our* advantage you know
Surely, you must understand, we have not changed purpose
We want the Middle East just as we want the world under us
Yes, we had the Jews go in to begin the conquering and slaying
Why we chuckle "Give it to a schmutz!" as we like to be saying
They too owe us, they took the atoms for peace, all they needed
And we cheer them on, couldn't wait until they succeeded.

Yes, Prometheus, nuclear fire, with its unearthly light is divine
And truly is appropriate for our Franken-offspring in Palestine
I'm sure you'd agree, but it's amazing to us that you don't see it
Our ubiquitous role in the world, but you haven't got the wit
It's not much of a trick, playing religion into electioneering
Harp on fears, while a managed press avoids quashes reasoning
Then add in spicy dashes of "us and them" as well we remember
And top with a Reichstag, some bad guys one day in September

We move on all fronts bleeding everyone multi-nationally
Thank God for the internet's porous financial boundary
Thank God for the corporation, the G7, and world bank
Thank God for simple ignorant investors settled file and rank
Generations deep, starting on the ground floor, as you put it,
This is prerequisite before any first move to make a gambit
Multi generations of war on untermenschen kept on the run,
Which has me reflect on your hapless Confederate Revolution

Even then you were being supplanted on your own ground
As our kind easily infused yours with cultural gains profound
Cheering on manifest destiny to cleanse the continent
Of the natives, the unions, democratists, and any discontent
So I tell you of our mal-intent, ill advisement and guile
We've been investing for generations, planning all the while
"It's not who votes that counts, but who counts the votes."
Credit lines pull the strings, puppets, choices, do take notes.

We handed you Russia, hobbled by Communist blunder
And through you kept England in hand and France turned under,
We were of the same mind so you didn't stand a chance
Of seeing through our masks – you, abyssal in ignorance,
Simply put, we destroy any competing human system
NATO, and the west our dangling puppet and asylum
We invented the fascism and the transnational business class
The Patriot Act drummed your freedoms into exile en masse

We've used your nation's resources for decades at this point
All over the world, in Africa where our missionaries anoint
But you don't see the pattern: whites killing those of color
Those of color set to kill one another – the cold war's horror
As a test population, the Moslem has been sent and spent,
But this no surprise; they hardly needed our encouragement!
So we've been having our little fun with them, that's our bag
At least that would be the lead story, if we had a company rag

By now, you wonder, why should we tell you this?
To that query, we say we wouldn't want to be amiss
That it is, after all, fair and expected, before any fatal blow
In both fencing and chess, to give warning to one's foe.
This is to allow them to be full aware of their intimate situation
To understand the need to for equal footing in the contestation
Everyone knows fair forewarning has God's justice prevail
So the better man shall win any fair contest without fail

In addition, we also feel that you've the right to make amends
To consider your situation, make preparation, tie up loose ends,
Take a moment for reflection before you meet your maker, do.
Now then, to all of those about to die for us, we salute you!

The Last Full Moon Of Peace *(08.09.06)*

It was a glorious full moon
During the ides of August
It was brilliant
The sky was over washed with its light
So the stars could hardly be seen
Only Jupiter stood watch
And Mars
As for Venus – I hadn't seen it that morning
I had a guess
That it was too ashamed to behold
Their grisly spectacle unfolding, no writhing
Amid the wrack and ruin of her dearly beloved Earth's
Sacred cradle of civilization

It was that high moon which was the last one I saw
Before the wars began in earnest
And so it is still sweet to me and its recollection dear

It was when those foes
Who had taken to the field
And set themselves warring with one another
Still had much in common
Each party believed it was aggrieved
That it was defending hearth and kin
That it had God on its side
Both felt they were in their game
That reality could be molded as easily as clay
And truth could be created by the loudest
And right belonged only to the strong
Or most willful

And, finally, both remained confident
Boasting and prideful of their self assurance
That they had control

And were capable
Of managing the spreading chaos to advantage
I speak to you now
As these foreshadowing guns of August bellow
Before the spreading shadows occlude
To overtake the souls of billions

Time is not on anyone's side
Nor, truth be told, does it seem, God is

There are no ships, which will bear us to safe havens
No reason to expect the hope I yet bear
Will flourish, blossom forth, and yield its wholesome fruit

It is a time of gathering gloom
Chilling shadows and dire moaning winds
Of bleak dusty landscapes
And furtive shadows

Fools call it The Rapture
Idiot pundits speak of chaos theory
Insane idolaters twist their illusions into feasts
Of flesh and spirit
As they pray – yearning for fearful prophesies to unfold

It is of no account that they are all of them deceived
So long as the truth of the matter remains hidden:
That the world is in our own hands
And it is we who have let its circulations fail
Loosed the reigns
On tides and migrations
Bid the seasons dance to new rhythms
And the rain to fall
Where chance
Or chaos allow
Furrows and plantings will not avail

Mother nature
And father time will see to that

It was a beautiful moon then
The gentle bay lay quiet before the eastern hills
The night air was warm, inviting

And we strolled beneath – in the pure silvery light
Commenting on the ordinary aspects of our lives
Reminiscing as if we had all the time in the world
And nothing better to do than laugh at a silly pun
Or take a little kiss

I will always remember how full, bright, and peaceful
The moon was that night
How soft the breath of wind,
Which had those beautiful ivory roses sway.
Their silky touch,
And wafts of perfume –
The last things I recall
From that night of the last peaceful full moon!

Hand To hand

He was elderly
That's what you'd call him
Still pretty tall, frail though
He had to be in his 80's
I happened to be there
And watched him walk steadily
Going toward The Wall
It was winter then
The cold white light peculiar to that season
Glowed upon him
And made his white hair,
Close cropped and thinning as it was
All the brighter

He wore a blue woolen suit
And a veteran's cap
Tied to the point at its back
Was a set of feathers
It had been these
And their dangling strings attaching them
That had caught my eye, at first

He went along a direct line
As he approached The Wall
Honoring the Vietnam War's dead
And so seemed to know
The exact point of his destination
He'd been there before   knowing

And he stopped, of course,
Before it and drew himself up
Took off his spectacles
Wiped them and placed them back on

I was on my own pilgrimage
And by then was not far behind him   to his left
I did not mean to intrude
So I hesitated, a moment, even as he seemed to

And took precautions
To keep my shadow out of his sight
Instead of moving on though, I remained   curious

He raised his hand and extended it slowly
To The Wall
As sunset colors washed their reflections
On its polished surface
I saw his hand's shadow approach the real deal

As reality and reflection met
He sadly looked down
Not at any particular name, I could see that
But staring, somehow away   into time
Into some place I'll never know
I heard him sigh
Noticed his lips in the barest of motions
Then, in a moment of quietude, I heard his murmur

Saw that he hadn't placed his hand on any one name
He was moving it along to new places
As if searching, blindly for something
I felt he was addressing them all
That this was his personal
And intimately mute wailing wall
I stepped away   I did not belong in his service
Was he one of the "old men" of that war?
Who is he hoping to touch?
What laughter was he hearing?
Whose smile does he miss still   after all these years …

I, on the other hand,
Had my own meaning to find from The Wall
My own ghosts to address

When he walked away
He went more slowly than when he'd come
And seemed a bit more stooped maybe

When he'd gone about twenty paces
He stopped, removed his glasses   wiped them
Took a deep breath
And looked beyond to the capital's dome
Before moving on

That's when I turned to face the wall
I touched it too   for my brother   for all the brothers
And the sorrow that yet breaks me down
From time to time
When a song plays
When a headline reads
When I am reminded of an immense lie
And how, tears serve, when nothing else does
To honor those who believed
That their sacrifice was worth its value

Memorial Day, 2010

Shall we mourn my friends;
Mourn ever anew and anon?
What say of this time and place?
Are we not men and women?
Do we not yet breathe?
Do we not have the trappings of freedom?
Wherefore are our rights?
Where the rage against this darkling?
What is a better time than now?
The better cause than this?
How now are we found wanting –
If not in the simple things –
Then certainly in all things precious?

And what is precious?
Could it be the right of anyone born here
To be guaranteed citizenship;
No matter the diabolical filth of Arizona
Finding wider acceptance?
Could it be the right
Of any citizen to exercise
Their freedom to worship;
To do so without fear of neighborly,
Or state-borne interruptions?

No matter Mr. "Old Gutless Wonder" McStain
Or Sarah "Miss Mattress Back USA" Palin's
So called "thoughts" on these topics

Does "the witless wonder"
Not know his republic was birthed with such ideals –
To wit: The Constitution, Article 6, "… no religious test shall
ever be required as a qualification to any office or public trust
under the United States … "

Does no one in Arizona
Or the Reich Wing Blabopsphere
Understand the law of the land?

The 14th Amendment, Section 1:

"All persons born or naturalized in the United States, and
subject to the jurisdiction thereof, are citizens of the United
States and of the state wherein they reside. No state shall make
or enforce any law, which shall abridge the privileges or
immunities of citizens of the United States; nor shall any state
deprive any person of life, liberty, or property, without due
process of law; nor deny to any person within its jurisdiction
the equal protection of the laws."

Peace

Create this once
And you've created it one thousand times
One million times
One thousand million never ending times
Peace is what is

Between any two thoughts
Any two breaths
Any two heartbeats   a stillness

Peace   is what is
Between the dreams
The wants and wishes a stillness

Peace   is what is
When nothing at all is happening
When the air is calm
As the gold of day
Settles into night's deepening hues there is
A stillness

Peace   is what it is   in this world
When the soul is unruffled
With a simple indrawn breath
Providing perspective before you simply react
When you look before you leap, as it were
And you keep   a stillness

Peace   is what it is
On a tranquil pond with reflections that mirror life
Until that first duck skids in   or a breeze wrinkles it
Creating an impressionistic collage
Of green and sky sequins

With   a stillness
Peace   is what it is
When each step is a forward step
On the path that lay easy before you
With a gentle wind at your back
And you walk along with   a stillness

Peace   is what it is
When your quietude is like that of the new moon's
As you're reeling with the inspiration of a lover's serenade
All on a lazy hazy summer's night
And each clear moving note
Is embraced by   a stillness

Peace   is what is
In harmony
It's the heart of the matter
And therefore of all matter
Of the universe   for all time   a stillness

Peace   is what is
When you create it
And   being that it is,
All there is
Peace is
A stillness

Create this once
And you've created it one thousand times
One million times   one thousand million never ending times
Peace is
A stillness

At Ocean Beach

Where November has been and gone
And the sun has long since set

The tide lay at its lowest
But the breeze, from the east,
Was surprisingly warm and gentle

I left my friends by the bonfire
Ambled toward the ranks of low, sweeping incoming waves
So their noisome talk was lost to the ocean's sound

Ahead of me ... after the waters withdrew,
There, on the wet moonlit strand
Was a star's reflection ... fading
As water subsided into sand

So I stood ... for a time ... as each watery phase waned
To see it shimmer ... close at hand

It was a light lost from its kind
Far, far from home
And everything it knew ... so it too ... was alone

Of course,
As I approached – it wandered
I could never reach it ... no matter how I might understand
Why it was where it was
Or how would remain but only relative to me
And so I smiled, for we were both touching our present
As if forever was never more ...
As timelessness measured my sigh

This ... fragile ... tiny gleam
Seemingly so still was touch of eternity

Which was fixed, secure, larger yet fading for all its glory
While this hint of something unimaginably distant
Was unreachable though but a scant few steps off

Behind me my temporal world awaited
My friends conversed
As the bottle was passed 'round
Lost in their kind of present
Which would soon become forgotten
After coming to be called the past
Which is to say, at the time their minds were through with it

As for the future,
Little star,
Someday … perhaps
They'll see, as do I
That although there are certainly differences
Between you and I in our existential extremes

I want you to know
As far as I am concerned
Right now … right here
On a balmy night such as this
After all is said and done
Those differences
Are nothing much to speak of
When compared to all we now have in common

****

Chapter Eight

11/8 – Present   30th Avenue

During this period I continued to attend open mics, began hosting the reading at Sacred Grounds, and became more interested in social change; something that had always been an interest but at this time, notably during the Bush Reign of Error, my attentions were drawn to doing more, becoming an activist in varied ways. I was never caught.

There are workshop pieces in this set along with inspirational and interior tapestries as well.

122

<u>*One*</u>

Love, Life, and Liberation

What Now?

In your   eyes
That time
There was the full moon

Now, we'd gone out
On a short walk
Taking in the night air,
Very late -- it was almost silent
As we went up Geary
Then found our way
To a quiet side street a few blocks north
Tree lined and hushed
We strolled
Slowly
Along

Such a simple time
I hardly
Expected anything
To come of it
Really

But there was this moon
And as we looked at one another
It was in there,
After one kiss, and
Before the next,
As we embraced
You said it was in my eyes …
And I said
"Oh, but it's in yours, my dear."
We did then fing
That its presence in both of us was
Unexpectedly funny

To My Love, Asleep And Dreaming

To my love asleep and dreaming,
Whose motioning lids seem but to presage
A message you would give me
From a time and place that knows no age.

There, I saw you gentled a'slumber
Taking rest as you may
And then you smiled gently
As you seemed to look my way.

Were you amused by what transpires
In your idyll dreams' moonset or sunrise,
Beneath those rosy lids of yours
Which must then comprise your skies?

For a moment   did I see?
Were they quick – and then still?
Were those precious orbs, your eyes,
Being directed by your will?

No sooner did this thought come
Then I presumed that you knew
I overlooked your slumbering form
As my silent appreciations flew

Gladdened as I was, I must add this –
Being painterly with words, some say
But shouldn't these reflections upon the truth
Be no less sweet she who inspired their play?

You beneath your blanket's languid folds
Adrift in dreamy forests, birds, and rainbows
Almost speaking, it surely seemed to me
Of misty bowers or sandy wading shallows

Standing by you in love with our love, my love
I wonder at the timeless miracle we've found –
Of how I speak to you with out a single sound
While your wordless reply is (holy) profound.

Several days later and all too far away
From that momentary bedside tableaux
I laughingly recounted this seminal event
Of which I hardly expected you to know.

You smiled coyly at this jewel of a memoir,
And then you gazed, and fondly so, upon me
What with other hints and your shift in repose
I was given to take your meaning, even if simply.

But you smiled in love, my love, you smiled
With your dear attentions direct upon me
And I smiled at your smiling and
My heart sprang joyful in its abiding love for thee.

No matter immensities, sundering mortal means,
Or illusions that birth simple, worldly doubt,
Or spells set to dun or sunder, it would be our hearts –
Miraculous – providing us Love's sweet redoubt.

And our good our faith flows through our love
So, even were we universes apart
We, would each still find the other
Through our perfect, sacred heart.

126

Some Promises

In the advisements from all those dearly departed
Unto we, the living
These items are listed, freely,
With no cost or expense for their giving:

Interdependent, in your age of machine,
Pushing both limit and bound,
You are never free from the temporal,
Abiding, and humbling ground.

Keep yourself fit, healthy and well,
And enjoy today's feast and jest
For no one knows when, why or how
They'll take their final test.

Take heed and care well for your family
And the friends you've known –
So that when hoary winds sweep wishes away,
You'll not be on your own
So through days of bitter enduring harvest you'll know
Just what it means to ever only reap
Exactly what it is you sow.

Keep your eyes, therefore, upon that eternal city
Of shining preternatural white
Above misty heights, 'neath sun and moon,
With its harbor of rosy light!

What A Puzzle!

Don't ask me about love
What a puzzle it is
Requiring hindsight foremost
The turning of a deaf ear or blind eye
Skin-deep vision
And sometimes   prerequisites
For example being stranded
Outside shivering and cursing the night's bitter cutting wind,
Counting on the silent pauses
Between gusts for their relative comfort of calm
Or being swept away
Bedraggled by a stormy whim … hopelessly hopeful
That something good will come of it   or
How fear palpitates
Through each thrust
Of the heart's blood
As it courses you onward
Toward what is true for it
And therefore real
Last … it is the finesse
The gasp, shuddering and deep ranging pang
When you behold all too familiar silhouettes in feeble light
As their amorous figures disengage from embrace
Yes … this would say it all … and far better than I ever could
As a prerequisite
For it speaks those volumes
Which the heart may
Which are, to one perspective,
Very little indeed,
Yet, in another,
Everything that matters in the whole world!

The Chance Of Who I Am

I am who I am by chance let no one gainsay that
With abundant proof clearly making my case quite pat.
My presence is a gift given me more than once to be sure
A string of pearly miracles and not just simple luck pure.
Once awakened by a thunderous boom and apoplexy
My eyes shocked wide to see I'd found my exit doing 60.
What hand guided mine while I was asleep at the wheel
Taking me to the off ramp during that unconscious ordeal?

Even where I now live was due to Mom's one-time yearning
To see the hills of her childhood and their colors turning.
Then, later, as a teen, being caught short in units of math
This supposed lack obviated Berkeley and led to this path:
Where amid SF State's tumult was it fate or "the force"
That I'd make a lifelong friend through poetical discourse?
Who later would reconnect through friends in common
And so provide an introduction to Golden Gate's Brahman?

Where in cycle and epicycle we danced amid mist and trees
With songs of God's love, incantations of heart's ease,
Or again, during a stroll, not a wish in my head
I met a friend from *The Walk* with she whom I'd wed.
So who was it that broke the afternoon date that day?
Or the messenger, which called that person away?
The paths one takes are interminably intertwined
With random access input from God's files chosen blind.

However said, this is justice at its simple and clear best
So when sitting in on life's session naught comes of protest.
Accept the arrangement, progressions of the composition
So when you are to take your solo – playing your rendition
You'll be subsumed in the tune and so make a hearty essay
No matter measure, your instrument, or how well you play.

One Road

A simple, small kitchen
Outside the back window
This piece of countryside
Is my friend's farm outside Salem
Besides enjoying the coffee's hum drum taste
I see winter's breadth
A slight blanket of fog covering the ground here abouts

Outside the back door
Dark, barren, overhanging branches   drip

A distant train … fades
My sight is drawn to the thickening overcast
The radio mentions blizzards
But static washes out the details

Sitting on the couch
My friend rustles the paper
Saying, "Redwoods are in the news again, and loggers … "
His wife dryly adds "Well, it's always worse in Portland."
It's her own in-joke but
It has me think of a friend who'd lived there – years ago
Before World War Two, when it was another world

The skin of my hands is aging and thin
I can see it clearly these days
Even now as they wrap around my warm cup
And I set to thinking about those finches
The ones that had taken up in the trees
Just beyond his property line
Fledglings and adults all chattering
We figured they were just stopping by
To rest up and feed if possible
We thought they'd stay the night but not much longer

For it was getting cold
And he thought they were off course and late
We saw them when we'd gone for a walk
And, not long after, in the neighboring field of stubble
A coyote loping along
Stopping here and there long enough to snap something up
It looked over towards us –
Or the houses a few times, checking

That afternoon, when I went out to get the mail,
It was as much to get in a walk down the long gravel road
As to do a mutual errand
It was cold enough for me
And the wind's scent was so rich
I thought it would snow soon

Suddenly a coyote appeared ahead of me
Trotting, surprisingly gaunt
He took little notice of me; he was pointedly intent
On making his oblique crossing of the roadway
Later, as a brief chill gust buffeted me, I saw him again
Ahead, on the roadside; he seemed to be waiting for me
When I caught his eye as he looked directly at mine
Not wanting to let him show me up
Or to deny his standing in the world
Or mine for that matter   I nodded
My ungainly crippled stride allowed him to dismiss me
Though he did look back once more
For whatever coyote reason he might have had

At my friend's place, after dinner
A clearing sky displayed the angelic realm
And a new moon's light
Glowed upon the clouds towering to the east
My friends had some business to attend to
And this allowed me to make my excuses …

And I took my leave. At our parting we were all quite jovial
Then, of course, I took the long way to my home
And walk by her place

Only, I mutter, to look at it
But I don't do that until after I've passed it by
Until I am just beyond that slight rise in the road
So when I do look back
It appears as if her windows are half buried
Beneath that immediate dark horizon line
All hunger, my Aunt said, is a gift,
So, even such as this, I guess, must be a gift
As surely as a nestled heart will wrestle with a truth
That its mind would deny
And my nearly stilled lips whisper
Something no one will ever hear
And nothing that will ever be repeated
Or ever forgotten, for all that

I wondered about those finches, though
Will they keep ahead of that front
Whose clouds amass towering just beyond the eastern hills?
Waiting for the season's command to move out
Bringing on their assaults of darkness and storm
Of moaning winds and slanted sleet
And a freezing night's bitter snow,
Which will settle into hushed drifts of deathly white
Bringing more desolation
To compliment that which I already bear

Crossing my threshold
I take solace in the hearth that I have – it will warm
Though it is now as still as my voice seems to be
And will be perhaps as long as I can't forget what never was
Or their laughter behind her warm glowing panes
When I approached through a forbidding cold that silent night

Only to find there was something colder
To strike at my heart
Which made snow all the less bitter, for such recollections
Later, finally, at home
Overlooking a nearly empty table – set for one
I offer myself some hope for this wasteful winter
Maybe the quieting silence of solitude
Will distract me from life as I would have had it
But which will never be

I light the fire and slowly pace about aimlessly
I watch my windows occlude
Courtesy of Jack Frost and fog
Until there is nothing much to see
Except my reflection set in shades of simple gray,
I take my rest then, turn to the flickering flames
And muse upon its changing shape and colors
The wriggling embers that trace fancies
And I hearken to those notes
Which come nearly of themselves
Tumbling my thoughts around
And all I have to do is listen to the rounds
Of a melody that, properly dreamt with,
Will become lyrics
Expressly in tune with it all
And how lovely is that?   I ask you?
How lovely   is that?

Listening In

1

Listening in
On the cycles
The wavelengths
Forming the warp and woof which comprise a matrix
That is the land and its forms
Which lay beneath me as I crest a small hill
And spend a moment overlooking the surrounding acres
Of an industrial farm of ripe seed grass
And beyond to the blue silhouette of Mary's Peak
And the plain June sky

Nearby
The Willamette catches rippled gleams
On this brightening day
When a deliberate osprey
Waggles above a spot … holding
Eyeing it
Before gliding down to make an easy catch
The fish wriggles for a moment … but that's all

2

Corvallis has its small shops and local's
It retains that hometown aura
Long gone from most places I know

As I stood at an intersection
Puzzling over the directions
The man in the old pick up
Gestures – to offer safe passage in the crosswalk
Later, an old couple nods to me in front of the drugstore
And others smile or quietly greet one another

It's a university town
A place honoring beavers
The legendary builders of this world

3

There are undertones
I feel through the soles of my new boots
From this farming valley
Which feeds few – if any to speak of – nowadays
I sense the thrumming flow of goods and services
The vital traffic coursing through the
Arterial and capillary streets
An effect of the relationships
Between persons, places and the land
It seems to tie everything together
And is part and parcel to the overlay
The orderly veneer
Which wraps the world into a neatly covered package
And is the magic carpet of civilization

We all ride upon it – and, in turn
Upon the sufferance of all that lay beneath it
The flooring, as it were
The foundation
Both of which lay forgotten
Though it has been only a few generations
Since we've come to believe
That this carpet is our foundation
That it is, in fact, all there is … to life

Such prideful footing
Has us walk upon that which we know nothing of
And so our cushioned lives
Can be as dream filled as we might like

Thus do we all dream a dreamer's life
No matter whether these be fruitful, pleasing

Wicked or nightmarish
We've a dreamer's life for all that
What use therefore is asking for the real time,
The alarm's setting
Or how early or late the hour might be?

4

What do I hear
From listening to the land,
The wind, the river
Or a flock of starlings
Mutely working southward
Through an afternoon's sky
Which both clear and brazen
Keeps our shadows small
And our comfort in disregard?

What do I hear
Beneath the slightest curve of a moon
Set in the cooling colors of the sky;
From the vernal spring's trickle
The creeks, which have slowed
The colorful river or
From the clouds gathering in the distance?

It is a silence,
Which says more than any "happy-talk" news
Or "doom-speak" prognosticator

It is the silence
Of factory farmed soil
That nothing crawls in or out of

Between browning stalks of seed corn
It is the silence in the trees
A gift of absent insects and birds
And the lack of anything moving
In the tall seed grass,
Which awaits only its machines

The fraying ecological fabric –
This hidden unraveling
 Ignores all things human

Silence
Found in the cold hard calculations
Graphing bell curves which are skewed
The shifting metrics used to analyze
Meandering ranges of flora and fauna
And the dry text of field studies
Which demonstrate how ecosystems rend
Dissolving into the chaos,
Which precedes their replacements,
It is fine formulaic math
The drawn out complexities
Which no super computer can number crunch

It is silence … then
Which answers my listening in
And
If we listen long enough to that
It will tell us all we need to know

Lyrics, In A Word

The most fragile off all things
Really
Tender and living … both
Taking and giving
Telling and not
The tales told by idiots
Sound bites and fury
News clips
Or reels
Reports on redemption
Rebirth
Soul searching embroilments
Heart rending imbroglios
Pain
Or dull, personal, long-term suffering
Sufferance
The slings and arrows of outrageous justice
The sins inherent in war
And then, too
The worlds of beauty – of nature
The nature of nature
Ah philosophy too
But the list is endless
These are the acts that lyrics cover

But Marilyn Monroe pegged it
When she said she liked poetry because
"… it saves so much time."
It shaves away
The frozen layers of perception
The crystalline matrix
Through which illumination can be seen
It is this which ever draws lyricists out and on and on
Toward the center

Is their cause, the reason they make that light speed
Hyperbolic turn shifting into another plane
To peel away that final filmy disguise
Even the one they know and love best
It is almost as well to deny fate
As to uncover the exact heart of the matter

That essence within every seed
Through which infinity unfolds – sprouting out everything
From its singular point of reference
It is the resource
That has ever been at the ready
In hand, as it were
As intimate as your every breath
As vital as each pulse

Which is why it is kept so dear
Why the muse sings in the manner that it does
Why it can whisper
Where so ever I go!

Wayfarer
The signal is clear
The frequencies are all open
You are in time and in sync
Warm up, tune in, and fly out
Home in … on the beam
Surf the only channel there is

I Sing

I'll admit it
Simply enough
Sometimes I whistle too
It's a bit odd
I'll admit that for sure
In this world of plugged in, interconnected disconnection
I am   a rare bird

Once, I was strolling downtown
When I noticed how intent everyone was
All around me they strode quickly along
Staring at screens, fingering figures
And, oddly, I was moved to whistle an old, old tune
I loved it   and knew the words but …
I could not bring my self to sing
I feared I'd be … embarrassed
But I couldn't say why, after all, who would hear?
It seemed that singing as one walks in a crowd
Is too interpersonal a thing
But whistling, well
Maybe not so much
Even then   it was still almost … crazy odd

Yet, there I was …
Whistling along
The only live performer in the midst of thousands
On a bustling downtown business district sidewalk
A musical mote among a work a day sidewalk scene
While everywhere I glanced the plugged in, interconnected
Dazed of eye, deaf of ear
And distracted of gaze
Were intent upon vibrations no one else was aware of
No sharing
No glances

No caring
Nor nods,
I could but watch
As I moved along through them
And so I was free to whistle away
Singing along to the song, in my mind, of course

I reflected on my resistance
To singing
As well as the satisfaction of whistling

Even as the throng
With its many, many widely varied people
On the strangely silent sidewalk
Each with their rigid face   determined and attentive
To something else, from somewhere else
Each   with far away eyes

None of them could hear me
And in that odd kind of public privacy
I could whistle on my merry way
Which I did
As much as I pleased

Though I dared not sing

This world's ending
Not so much a concern
As what comes next!

A Dream On The Beach

I dreamt I was playing guitar …
I don't
I knew that
But it was a beautiful day, really
I was under a canopy in warm shade with a bunch of people
Although I couldn't recognize anyone
I knew they were my friends
It was a party
They were happy with me as I entertained them
Far off couples strolled up and down
Along the midnight strand
Farther out waves rolled up from their turquoise field
Only to crumple into chaotic lines of white
Before each lazily then swept in over the sand –
Far beyond the hazy blue sea misted into the horizon's sky

And I mean I could play
And was thinking about how I'd change this progression
Adding in this or taking out that
As I listened to conversations
Others who sang along softly – not being sure of the words

I noticed how my calloused fingertips placed themselves
Pressing onto sharp, hard steel strings
They danced upon 'em like crazy spiders
I had to laugh at the conga player
Every time he nicked in with rhythmically humorous asides

Then, without looking, I knew she was there too …
I heard her … laugh
I imagined her beautiful smile,
Glistening auburn hair
And her bright … lively brown eyes gleaming happily

Conversations meandered
As I took requests, played them as they were called
Even if I had to make wild ridiculous segues
Quite a time, quite a time
I sang too
But it was in a language I did not know

I sang for free
For peace
For love and
For hope.

The drummer played off, on, and with me
But I never saw him
I had a wonderful time
I wish you were all there; you'd have loved it dearly
So I lingered
Watching this happy world
Fade before my eyes
As I eased back into this one
Which is quite different

Here it is winter – chilly winds sound outside
And cold rain taps at the sill
I did have presence of mind though
I slapped down the alarm before it went off

All that gray, dreary day
I had some hint of a smile every time I thought back
And felt a touch of the warmth
From a better, a gentler kinder place
A world, in fact, of beauty
One such as this one's troubled and wearied denizens
May only dream of

They Call It Singing

For miles around there is farmland
But I stopped to look at you
A great but lone tree
Of a kind I do not know
But which has long taken root here
In the soft love of the great mother
Through the parade of seasons

Your leaves seem golden in this light
And you whisper
Your limbs motion
So the thousands of leaves
Follow in millions of ways
This is your body
Singing
No wonder children love to come near
And regard you as a friend

Home to any bird
They join in with you
Though they play tunes of feast or drink
While you sing only of time

I took a portion of this day
To touch you with peaceful intent
Give you a pat
Speak softly and,
In a way, offer to you the grace I feel
As my beautiful eyes behold your elegant naked frame

The friendly wind plays soft
Through fluted clouds drifting in the sky
And you have a beautiful style
Wonderful taste in friends

And your mind refines mine
Your spirit laughs with the ground
And this is freedom
Intimate with our mother
You reach to the stars with muscular limbs
Moaning in your passion
So that God is pleased
His hands find your soul
And feels its yearning to build music

We share instruments you know
We are companions on this earth
And with it so are we friends of the sun and its planets

Mountains and clouds envy your dance
As they might my legs or tongue   were I among them
And singing as I do now, hopefully, with you
As you   dance

So, there'll be no sleep tonight
And I have become a pilgrim
With the whole of this prairie as my summer house
And it's true, Love does bring out the Truth
That one is never forsaken
As one may be   by the joys of our simple paths ...

Surely, my friend, we can guide each other here
Find what's hidden
Forever   when all we have is time

That night   heaven lifted its filmy veil
Revealing the magnificence of myriad worlds
Flung out upon the universe
Of unlimited Love
And our conduct of that Love was exemplary!

On Poetry

Poetry leaves no vacancy
No stone unturned, as it were
No space unexplored
No assumption untested
No theory is let to rest simply upon its laurels

Truth is not shy
So you may as well get over it right now
And surrender to the inevitable

Let the loving experience
Of everything there is
From the rich mantle of life coating our wondrous globe
To the vast glittering mysteries set in the jet of its surround
Come to you
Gently
In your dreams
Into your heartfelt soul

You see, in every breath you exhale
Or child's spoonful of soil
There is, in truth, something universal
Something of God
And so   something of you

Likewise
Cup your hands and take up seawater
In such a universe are endless dancers cavorting
Who, drunk on life,
Have found that this is all there is to need
They do not need intelligent reasons to revel
They do not need to know what sanity is
And of course love is ever on their minds
Although we cannot see those partiers

Hear their music going on twenty-four seven
Three sixty-five
They are there   and pumped up with ecstasy!
There are   then
No empty spaces

No place where there is only darkness
There is no loneliness
To those
Clear of eye
Sound of soul
And who, so in love with love,
As to joyfully laugh even at death's extremities

And this
This takes us back to the very beginning

Poetry, my dear friends, leaves no vacancy

No heart untended
No love withheld

    And no tear

       To fall

          Alone!

Reflections

Just as water slipped off this moonlit strand
One star's reflection – lay close to hand
Fighting the ripples – it seemed fraught
As if in fearful struggle against being caught
When the waters settled into the grains
Its light faded into their dark remains
I kept station awaiting the sweeping sheen's advance –
Expecting a reprise – of its unsteady dance

The water returned to overtop my shoes this time
Leaving upon them both sand grains and rime
But I saw it, I saw it near to me, I saw it there
Just as I noted a leak in my elderly boots wanted repair
To catch this note from far, far away I decided to stay
I studied its shimmer – as if it was a personal display
Considered the long cold journey evinced by that dot
And how we came to be … on what became our spot

The wind was coming from the west that night
And while it was steady it was only slight
Yet it bore a sweetness I would have otherwise denied
For she came to mind, as did regrets and I sighed
But as I stilled my body my mind wandered all the more
Began turning the pages of my life's storied lore
Took a trip touring the vistas of my yesteryears
As I stared at this light and felt a few tears

Only the silent moon gave its witnessing glow
To that which I would never otherwise show
But I was alone and so passions could be spent
As I looked on to the light which kept me … intent
I did not have the satisfaction of a heart warm in its bliss
Rather the benefits of spendthrift ways gone amiss
I longed to mend that which should never have been rent

The precious evolution of a love, which was transcendent
And here was a glimmer of light in that water so near
Which, in touching my soul, became love's souvenir
And while it could be said the star was nothing at all
Still it became something for me; it had meaning withal
No matter its silence or the grace of its wavering light
And that it could not know what it inspired that night

Ages upon ages, come as this or all recollections must go
While ever to the present do the timeless times flow
And so did I wait upon this anonymous star's light
As we both reflected, in depth, late that one summer's night

For the longest time
A blazing chunk of wood
Has eyes   nostrils …

In the small storage room,
I lovingly call "the office"
I sit at my desk.

When its window is open, as it usually is,
I see our modest garden
Of chard, green onions, broccoli, and leeks,
When they've been watered
Morning light will gleam upon leaf and stem,
Glint in the dark earth,
And today I note the lettuce seedlings
Getting their blush on
And the carrot tops are now inches in height.

There are bird calls from the wild backyard to the south,
And a delicious inflow of cool air,
Rich redolence of soft, green, freshness –
I close my eyes in reverie.

Beyond the yard to the south
Comes the sound of children at play
And, then, it being Tuesday, at noon,
There's the well-regulated siren
With its message
From the Emergency Broadcast System

I recollect, therefore, duck and cover drills,
Skies filled with a siren's blare.
And being trained to freeze where I stood.
Later, as I grew up,
I'd still glanced around for cover,
Wondering if a parked car would do?
Or try to make it down some basement stairs?
All while having no idea
Where the blast would come from,
Or if I could even be safe

From a sky set ablaze in the blink of an eye.
For years
I dutifully waited for the "All Clear."
Then, on this day,
Much as on many others
There came moments of wonder
Afterwards,

As to what I'd do
After the blast
If I weren't dead that is,
You know,
To tell the truth,
I never had much of an idea,
Back then, or even now.

But those childhood memories fade
As I look out a simple window
At a common garden,
Hearing the children play;
Children who do not
Duck and cover
Who do not know why the siren sounds
What it means.
To me
Or most anyone
Now-a-days …

My Table Of Contents

My friends and what they'll say about me when I'm gone
What I'd say of them at that time if I had the chance to
My family and what they'll say
My family and what I'll say they'll say
What we'll argue about and who'll get the last word
Getting back but good
Lying, stealing and cheating – at cards – to say the least
Taking it with a grain of salt –
Or getting hit with a whole damned salt lick
The Giant Dog That Scared Me Shitless
Nightmares I'll never forget
Hobbies and Habits I Hide
Annoying habits of others that I know I do
What a garden means to me
Ideal walks in idyll
Cooking – Dan's style
Humor: set jokes and upset jokes
Pissing in the wind
Pissing on, pissing off and being just plain pissed
My most infamous farts
Believe me when I say … even you can raise a ruckus
Just using your big fat mouth
Rumor Mongering, Backstabbing and Black Ops at work
Easy and not – going that is – the BIG difference …
Memories of Mom, Tom, John, and of friends departed
People younger, far younger than I, who died – stupidly
My 30th High School Reunion – the OMG outtakes
What I think I think God thinks – and who cares
Why I would not want to be God, the director's cut
On meaning what you say … and saying what you mean
My Grandiose schemes: A Political Party Platform
Ten easy ways to make a trillion dollars – for fun and profit
If they would only just listen to me and do what I say!
Sudden Human Extinctions, the fun possibilities

Eternities and Philosophies – big deals
How to take it from the slap
Slapping and being slapped; an illustrated history
Theosophical considerations
Poetry – and more poetry
Delving into Haiku, but just for a moment
Who I think I am and why
Why I think I am and who

What does anyone think of that and why
The just plain why – of all whys

The short and long of committee meetings …
What CAN happen in a minute
What does it matter?
What does anything matter?
What matters?
What is the matter?
Why is it that matter, more and more, matters more?
Just asking …
Kiss and tell
What the hell … ?
You do the math
The top ten reasons to get off this planet – and fast …
"Please" "really" and "I hear that," quotes and back stories
"Leave me alone, just go away, don't bother me."
My famous and infamous quotes that I don't like at all
And yes, I was drunk when I said some of those things
Anonymous Quotes by Famous People,
The unedited version, and
How to make a list poem out of nothing: "What the hell."

It Grows Fonder …

In your absence … John
I find space … to fill
Memories to question
Alleged hints to mull
An attitude to adjust, and more …

In a recent dream
I was in a large park in a picnic area
Walking an aisle between old fashioned green picnic tables
Perhaps a reception, everywhere there were knots of folks
As I went along, taking in the view and I saw you sitting
Hands, in easy fists set on the table thumbs up
With a generous platter set in front of you
Which you relished to no end
Sunlight on your face
You looked so much younger
And were earnestly talking to someone
Forgive me now for not saying hello
And forgive me for all I may have said or done
That wronged you

You passed six months ago
And today, as I strolled on my way home,
In a favored pair of raggedy old blue jeans
On a bright, very warm, March day
I noticed the trees along my street – as if for the first time
John, they are very same kind
As those which lined our childhood's street
The bark, its color, texture, and leaves –
How could I have not seen it?
And … when the wind came up, gentle … sweet
It was deliciously cool
Just as in those idyllic summery
In our merry old days of yore

There was a shift   in my world
As if a new center of gravity
Had gently   but firmly
Clunked   unto place
I thought about history

How, at one time or another
We were each other's heroes
"Way back east" as we used to call it
Long before we lost touch and track
Over all those ages before we were suddenly … torn apart

I looked up into this memorial of leaf and branch
Saw a radiant point glint amid shifting verdant shapes
And it became something new
And, so, to those of you receiving this
Take heed, now and again,
Regard the touchstones of your life … and do more
Respect the earth itself
Be kind to everyone you can
Brothers and sisters alike … for we all pass along
Never knowing when it will come about   or how – or why
With any one of a number of reasons
Being reason enough – to take us each out
When time goes – there are echoes – a pause in reality
Not silence – not an absence – not nothing …
Nor a sense that less is more

Whenever we are reminded that we too will go
That our intimates will forget
As gaps open – spans stretch and yawn
As they will when they leave   as their others forget them
Who will then … sense … the slight … pause feel … see
A shifting in the light   as I did
Bedazzled by a point of brilliance –

In which memoirs found me
Both of us –
John, together again,
Brave on a bright day eternal times ago
Believing in brotherhood's faith
And I began singing through the heart of our minds
But   in my soul   I was still
Cooly quiet as if of the grave – thought not, surely that yet
But more so than I was, a few minutes before
More than I will be a few moments hence
Knowing I am not yet freed of a burden
I had forgotten that I'd carried

Their flight   over stubble
A murder of crows   turn slowly
To circle above me

156

Big John

When a man dies
Who feels what is missed, who cries?
And who says   words   which must be said –
And who may feel all the lesser for his being dead

Who rises in respect as he makes his final cut?
Who, knowing him well, speaks of his why and for what?
Of the sod we both were yet he fought for our clan
While I hid thoughts, the works of my heart and hand

I mourn for him all the more for what's become of our land
Where inalienable rights lay beyond commoner's command
While no one yet tells me what I can or cannot write or say
They do go 'roun' takin' names; and stealing dreams away

There are those whose industry would take the sky from me
Those that mock the choked gasping of our Lady Liberty
Others that profit as they stifle the land or suffocate the sea
As their minions connive to hide their lies from the likes of me

John, I know, is here in this place, no matter that I can't see
He's borne in our hearts and part of our long family history
And yes he has journeyed as will we each someday – and I –
I will follow answering when called up into the all-eternal sky

Which?

Which died the better?
John or Tom
Presenting them in the order of their deaths …
Tom died first, over 40 years ago now
The shrapnel
From a mortar round caught him out
He had been accounting for their rate of fire,
Timing his sprints,
Advancing on their position – his platoon pinned by fire
He would have killed them all   had he had the chance
Yet luck ran out … Tom died instead

John came home from the war
Different, of course, and sometimes coarse, of course
He was my best man,
Offering the toast I can still see and hear today
Who, having survived the war,
Worked his way along in his life
Taking on a woman's love and that of her child's too
He made a difference for others … many others …
As a policeman, a driver, a brother, father, and grandfather
But, bitter at the legacy of war, rarely spoke of it
And I never asked
I believe he longed for comprehensive peace

Then, one fine day, he found he was dying
And that there was nothing for it
His last battle was with the side effects of Agent Orange
He made appointments, had conferences
Continued to work out and swim
Muscling into his famed routines
But still … after hard surgeries … hallucinations
Faced down damnation when it came to call
Before they had to crack open his chest; leaving great scars

That never had the time to heal
As it turned out …

Once he held out his hand to me
Asked me to pull him into a sitting position
He wanted, ultimately,
To stand on his own two feet once more
And was so damned pissed off
As I tried, we tried, straining hard,
Sweating and coloring up
But he did not rise to that occasion
And, fearful, both of us,
Agreed it had been a bad idea from the start

Still   death came

And I saw him go … but he did not, could not, see me
As the indicators dropped
And the silence dragged on with the flat line

So … which died the better?
The worse?
The wiser?

I began this as something else clearly
But now … I reflect … restudy
What has come to me after all these years
The choices they made, which I couldn't have
The considerations I had which they did not
How their patriotic volunteering caught me unaware
And how unprepared as I was
For both of their ends
Still   I wonder
Which died the better?
The worse?   The wiser?

The Last Word:

No matter how far you've gone,
Or where you've come from
It's a place that lets you in
It was a Midwestern Bible hot day
We were driving cross-country, my sister and I
And had pulled off to this town
Which was small enough to holler across
And get back talk from both sides

There were no fences between the houses
The streets were paved, of course, but quite worn
The big buildings were the elementary school
The retirement home
And, just at the off ramp, there was the "Big Deal"
A mini mall combining a motel, restaurant, corner store
Gas station, bookstore, and bar
The "Big Deal" fronted for the town
Which was a quarter-mile up on the two lane

All around the place grew the corn – rolling hills of corn
This was in Iowa, the center of our nation … the continent
I thought the land was too sullen
Something about it was suspicious,
Maybe because it was so wide
Also it was to quiet, I thought, even for a village

Judging from the few regulars at the small café
People weathered fairly well
The waitress was friendly and, from the small talk,
Everyone knew everyone else's business
Judging from the courtesy conversation
My sister and I enjoyed
We believed they believed in being kind to strangers

After eating we walked around.
Some of the homes were over a century old and looked it.
The chief downtown attraction was the Old West Theatre;
Where events were on the calendar
Prominently placed in the window

But it was old, nonetheless
It's claim to fame was Bill Cody's visit

This was a farmer's town – each porch was just as tidy
As if a visit were expected

Big trucks were parked in small graveled driveways
Flowers were in planters fronting every porch
And each little garden fence had cute frilly trim
As did most porch railings front windows and doors

There were children's toys in the yards
No one here thought they had to take things inside
I guess the worst thing that could happen to them was rain
After all, this was a simple place
Of shade trees and flower plots
At the very calm center of these United States
Far away from any coastal anxiety or distant rumbling

My sister figured it for "A nice enough place"
And I had to agree, I even said, "Yes, yes it is."

But we left, for all we knew, never to return
For we were on a journey that bore us
Through our memories and recollections onward
To family and friends
As we drove past forgotten horizons,
We both held some our dreams
And wishes out for consideration

As for the reflections,
Those that we'd never admit to each other,
To say nothing of ourselves
We both left such up to the tender mercies
Of both time and love
Trusting they'll give them their airing in due course
Before this journey,
We had gone many long years between laughs
Even to our most ancient of times
It will be the gales of laughter that I'll recall, especially
When memories such they are all I'll have left
And while they will certainly not be enough,
All things considered
I'm sure they will do
Thank you Kathy
For every single laughing matter

Picnic   two toddlers
On their gingham field   dance
To Gerschwin's jazz

Before I Become 60 ...

With 60 years I have been blessed
I have borne each winter's test
Passed through intervening vales of grief
And now seasons pass flickeringly brief

Betimes, in comfort, I recall childhood's happy dell
The high tide of my youthful pride's swell
And how, with my majority obtained – I waxed
As I chose doors, paths, paid tolls, and was taxed

How now does my mirror provide reflections dour
And how oft does death's gentle touch but hint at its power
Just as endless night, above the cerulean, is known to hover
As if nothing I say or do could provide safe harbor or cover

Yet as I settle into curving dunes amid lush grasses to gaze
At the encroaching fog I reminisce upon ancient salad days
When red blooms unfolded with precious dews divine
While here waves rush in to measure both sands and my time

There's no a chance the Pacific will change however I rage
The shore will advance, regain losses, and make a new age
Or that, one by one, my mystical friends, gone so very long
Will dance by bonfire's light to drum, flute, and song.

So I whisper to heaven grant whatever years I may yet hold
That I'll be allowed a lightness of heart and vivacity bold
And a spring to my mind, if not in my step – and the sight
To view the fog of life as veil, not a shroud, occluding light!

163

Two

History, Memoirs, and Hope

Haiku instructions
Cut to the chase, home in
And get the hell out!

Glory

Of glory I write   and flags
And more
Of causes so great
As drive the chariot of war
Of banners and pennants
And the crimson on their cloth
Bugling, fifes, and ruler's wroth
Of those brightly young
So handsome, so whole, courageous and strong
Of the surety they couldn't possibly be wrong
Of glory I write
And flags and more
Of marching and pride
Of bullets and gore

In these deepening days we live in a pall
Battle is now modern, not simple at all
The world of war has changed of late
For pride has waxed – it's now globally great
As are the sins of ignorance, greed and hate

Race and culture still play their parts
As do philosophy, economics
And the sacred beliefs held in men's hearts

So no thing is left that could be called clean
All is sullied by that "Midas Touch" and has become mean
Every hand has its own form of that damned stain
Every dream has been taken and turned into pain

Of glory I write and flags and more
Of stories told to children
Which lead them on to war

As do those songs and verse of overweening glory too
And legends of god like acts – more than a few
The man who struck three hundred down dead
The three hundred who stood off a tide of a million instead

All the spit and polish that swells a heart with pride
All the boasting fools on any fighting side
So we're in "interesting times" as more hear the cry
As they rush answering the call never questioning why

Would that the world give up its torturous dread
As has made human history so drippingly red
That has cut the yield of promising lives
Who then march along with their damned honored dead

So mothers will weep and lovers moan
While fathers walk it off and sigh alone
Yet, millions don uniforms today as before
So millions more will die evening their score
While further millions all cheering wish them well
And this will continue until that rough beast falls into hell!

Martin To Me

There's an old spiritual about bearing the burden
As I heard it I wondered about you, Martin
What scars remain still – after all these years?
The sharp-eyed folks who cut you
Drawing lines, at first with hate …
And, finally, afterwards … with love
But the eternity in one angry face had you polish the basics
Your breath … your voice
It's why your words find my heart these days
And declare, after all these years,
That you are "the man"
The broad back that carried forth a new generation
And when you came down from the mountaintop
Declaring to the crowd, "I might not get there with you …"
You knew whereof you spoke
And I believed you … all those years ago
When you talked about the promised-land
Or when you wrote of God's love in that solitary cell
All those years ago
About 20 million brothers and sisters
Suffocating
For want
I believe it was those considerations
That stared you back in the eye
Each day when you first looked into the mirror
Which became a signature moment … to say the least
The meditative prescript
A reflective introduction … the preface
For what became your daily practicum:
Which was the belief that each day was your very last

And yet you bore it well
Took your faithful passion into an American kind of hell
Bearing its light

And hallelujah banners through the darkness
Of solidified and stolid, sweating, white hate
Walls of eyes upon you
You spoke
All those years ago

I have to ask, who can live that way?
Think about it what would your first order of business be?
What pledges would you make?
What actions would you take?
What manner would your address to others be?
Would you give it up and let your fortune go for free?
To what ends would your every breath be spent?

And so I fail before such a comparison
I cannot live each day
As if it were my last
Yet this is the challenge you present
Your eyes ask, do we not hear the same call?
Your hands gesture, do we not still breathe free?

How then, brothers and sisters
Do we answer that clarion?
The birth of light in the heart of man
And the gift of what means to be human
Brilliantly shining
From ever joyful eyes
Which is what I saw
All those years ago
When you spoke
Of having been to mountain top
And having seen the promised-land
On that warm and final southern night

This piece is from my first book, "Orphan City", written for those coming of age in this wild and crazy time of ours.

I have a history
I come from a people
Who do not know their name
Who do not tell their stories
Who do not know their tongue
Who cannot hear their songs

Who do not sing
Who do not dance their dances
Who do not know the names of their stars
Who cannot eat the food they find here
Who cannot grow their food
Who cannot take what is given as value
Who do not understand the thinking of this place
Who cannot have the kind of houses that live
Who cannot be brave and do good
Who cannot make their way in this world
Who are ignored – left aside
Called names … hidden … kept invisible
Lied to, lied about, lied with, for, and against
I come from a people
A people who have lost their love
Who have lost their land
Whose language is not written
Whose words are not read
Whose reason for being is questioned
Who are measured
Who are counted
Who are not allowed
Who do not own
Who do not have

Who are asked for more … and who are looked at funny
Who are suspected, rejected, injected, and selected
And who, after all of that unending trial
Who don't have a way to be and who are then asked
Why don't you care?
I am not what I wear
Not my Nikes
I am not my gender
Not a boy
I am not my ethnicity
Not an Arab
I am not my religion
Not Muslim
I am not my nation
Not American
I am not what I eat,
Rice and veggies,
I am not my school
Not my classmates
Not my test scores
Not my beautiful eyes
Not my smooth skin
Not my music
Not my books
Not my laughter
Not what you can see
Not what you can touch
Hear, talk about, learn about
Say about me
I am not anything you can measure
I am not what you think when you see me
I am not seen
Not heard
Not known for what I am
Seen for what I love

The Western Wind

Night … looking west from Ocean Beach
Waters lay … unusually peaceful and calm
The many waves … small
The wind sweeping by … steady … strong

Far, far away …

It rushes … crowds my ears
I hear nothing else
It dries my eyes … so I blink
As they water in response

Occasionally
A sand grains sting my skin
Tap my windbreaker … or hat …

There is no happiness here

Then … in the shushing s
I believe there are whispers
This is because I do not know where you are
Or why you have gone
Which is why, for some reason,
I came here
To stare out over the great Pacific
And into the far more vast sky of stars

And there is no moon and I am glad of that
At least one thing has gone right

Entangled with sorrow
Which weighs more than I would have thought
Such is the blindness of joy
And the wonders of that timeless time … of love

Strolling … I chance upon letters left in the sand
Nearly obliterated by the waves
But I avoid looking as soon as I noticed them
A young and athletic woman jogs by … her hair flying
Her footprints smash along through the remaining line
And so there is chaos
And regret for not letting curiosity have its way

But then another wave runs in and sweeps it all away

There is nothing left
No one in sight
No one to hear what I would say
If I could say it

Even my own sigh is taken by the wind
Its warmth … lost
Its reason for being … its trace
Lost forever
Its water vapor carried off
To someday join in with the clouds
To prism the glory of the sun
And bless a sunset … somewhere

And that's all there is to it …

There is nothing more to tell …

So it goes …

So it goes …

Light And Shadow Plays
Reply to William Cowper's "Light Shining Out Of Darkness"

However dark darkness may seem
A light yet shines throughout its dream
God's mystery moves in such wondrous ways as this:
Even in abyssal deeps one finds mercy's gentle kiss

Titans may stir with their strident footsteps
Rousing the seas to swarm
With such turbulent waves
As have them sweep beyond their ocean's form,
Antediluvian demons may forge,
In the mines with their unfathomable passion,
Such elemental horrors
As only their hellish crafts and skill could fashion –
And they'd set these baleful, nightmares,
These misshapen soulless beasts
To fall upon us, gnawing flesh off our living bones
At their gruesome feasts
As a dreadful, darkling sky
Pours a hateful poisonous rain
Forbidding of any earthly thirst
And sears any wanting tongues with pain
Yet through that sky of roiling smokes
A golden merciful beam will break
And all would feel its gentle promise,
Which no one could mistake

Even such a world as that, or ours,
Is not beyond the Sovereign's will
Forsaken not, our immortal souls
Are kept forever peaceful still
It's the hope of this that bears us through,
It's a treasure well designed
For through such faith

Even fearful saints will their courage find.
Such hope smoothes the furrowed temple
And cools the feverish head
A blessing of our trust in grace –
Which the Lord provides us in our stead

Though vast and frowning ill providence
May test us fast and fair
Still, beyond earthly woes, eternally,
His smile regards us with care

Through His single never-ending hour
His purpose ripens within us here
Unfolding with each trembling beat
Of our fleshly metronome, so why fear?

No matter then, the acrid essence
Of a burgeoning bud's first taste,
When such portends the sweetened flower
That fruits fulfill with lack of haste
Unbelievers are blind to the future's gift
And so live only to err or waste
And, knowing not but what they do,
Leave a life and all in its wake – debased
And while some others might study
Until every holy work has been scanned
All they'll glean is what has been writ
By someone else's eloquent hand
Surely you can see how such efforts
Are unfortunately spent in vain
For such scholars will not be blessed
With His greatest pleasures or gain
It is to the beneficent –
Those whose love and gifts are given free –
Who'll receive that bounty, a measure of faith
A grateful God provides the loving devotee

The Dunes

1

On the dunes   I see sand ...
At my feet
The rills slowly shift eastward
In the slight constant breeze
There is a steady, gentle movement of grains
These create shifting sparkling constellations
As their minute prismatic facets catch and glint
I know, were I to stand here, patiently
My shoes would soon be over washed

It has been a long, long time now
Many things have been covered over
All I can see here now are the dunes
There is nothing of the landscape that once was

When I was born people lived everywhere
I recall it easily enough, the teeming millions in the cities
Nations, highways
And living what we called, a "life style" back then

2

When a person becomes ill
A fever is consequent
Normally a matter of a few degrees
The body's temperature is part of its defense

But add a few degrees more and it cannot survive.
It is a small difference
That between normal and fever and
That between fever and death

The world of ours … as it is now
Has gone beyond a simple fever
It was a matter of a few degrees, really
The 10 degrees of separation … was the joke back then
Back when there was still an illusion of hope
Before a cascade of failures

The surprising speed of the polar melt
Rising oceans
And the collapse of the ecology
The loss of continental glaciers, even big rivers drying out
Desserts spread
Rain patterns shifted
The climate … shrugged us off
With hurricanes, tides – even earthquakes

It was alarming how quickly so many perished
There were diseases, yes, some new ones too,
Which caught everyone by surprise
And then, of course,
There were the wars   all ultimately petty and foolish
No … worse … wasteful and horribly so
For they were all inconsequential
Now that their nations are ghosts

3

The shifting sand beneath my feet tells me this … and more

Now
This place is over … the sand is drifting in
And we are moving out … again

We've heard there are still trees far to the north – even forests
That there are seasons up there
And we also hear there is fighting, but that's no surprise

I am from the old days
The few children ask for stories
Some of the older ones, the young adults now
Take notes, keep records
For we have not lost everything

We still know how to think
How to hunt   how to harvest

Buried cities will one day be unburied
The machines and magic of a bygone day will be puzzled over

But such will not be in my time
I have tried here and failed to hold on

Perhaps leaving them with the legacy of literacy
Is the only boon I can pass on

That and a hope that the world will change again
And that we'll return to the lands
That once had names   places that spoke of history
And succeed where our people, in the past, failed

Sometimes I remember friends
Occasional places, memories
They come unbidden and are unwelcome here
For they pain my heart and bring on tears

When my people see me in such a state
They grow quiet
For they cannot mourn what they do not know
And I cannot forget what they'll never see

Baseball's Diamond

Translucent high thin overcast
Blurs the suns disk, which appears silvered
And cold in the grey wash of winter sky
The ides of November –
I walk this old baseball diamond, over and over
Speculating as to where the bases should be
When only home remains, fixed, bolted into the earth.

The chain link cage behind it is still good, but rust colored.
And the thick green paint on the backboard is hardly faded.
I can make out the tracings of posters or signs
None are legible
Behind the backboard there was a water faucet
Which, of course, I didn't bother to try.

I walked to the pitcher's mound
Scuffed into the soil and was surprised to find its marker
I sized up the distance home,
Imagined a play, the curving flash of the ball to the plate
That unmistakable punctuation
And the white sphere's arc into a blue sky.
The catcher, throwing back his cap
Tries for it, leaping out –
Slips and falls to the dusty earth
But gets that throw in to first,
Where the runner just slid through clouds to safety.
I see the runner stand and clap off dust   and smiling
Then, eyeing me, the pitcher,
The next batter, and the third base coach
He takes a lead, hoping to steal second.
Yes, a tight game.
But there's no schedule or innings posted,
No picnic blankets, applause, warm ups, hand signals,
No stinging smack in the old glove –

None of the trappings no hint
No trace of players, or tallies of wins or losses –
There is no one in sight of this old place.
No one to be embarrassed by or for
Just the hills and distant trees.

And I stand uselessly on an icon of a bygone day.
A sudden wind's chill smells fresh,
I think there'll be rain by nightfall.
And then, because the grasses are brown in the outfield,
I approve.

A five-minute walk from here
Is the abandoned house I've moved into
I look up and guess that I'll get back before the rain breaks.
Holding that belief even as a few fat drops splattered
And I could smell the ozone in the gusts sporting about me.

Who'd have thought there was a field anywhere around?
And in such good shape –
Looking as though it could be made ready
It wasn't too overgrown,
Give it a good rain, then,
After a week or two, I could mow it
Rake the infield, chalk it all out
Fix some bags in place
And wait for the pick up games to start.

It could be done – I could do it
But who would come to play?
Certainly the other houses in the area
Have cellars stored up like the place I have
And there could still be people,
Then too it has been a few months
With nothing much left of what was
And while I don't know who let darkness fall

Or how I lucked out to survive
I do know I'm not at all that anxious to find anyone anyway.
On the one hand what would I say
What would I want to say – what would it matter?

We're social animals
So when society is gone
There's no context for any act to have meaning –
It used to be that everything was political
Now, nothing is, nothing can be without a polity.

It's been weeks since I went to the bluff
Overlooking the interstate
And saw that one pick up
Pulled over, abandoned, its hood up.
Then spied on that other town with a telescope
Saw several cars in motion and heard gunshots

So I hold up here.
Don't keep lights on, drive, use electricity,
Or make smoke,

What's wrong with staying anyway?
Maybe the baseball field should be fixed up,
Tended, made welcoming.
Someday we'll have a team here, a local league.
Wouldn't that be something?
And wouldn't that be just like me?
Lost, unknown, doing the useless, for the forgotten,
And caring all the more, as well as nonetheless …
Therefore I will start tomorrow – early
Bright and early, after flap jacks
Good coffee and beans.
But tonight, tonight as the cool air settles,
And the summer is whisked away,
Tonight I'll plan.

One Small Step ...

It was a time of dreams
When hope   like never before had everyone looking up

All around the world they said, "We did it."
Not, Americans   not "they" but "we"

It was such a time   as we saw what we could do
Saw the fragile and singular
Blue, white-brown, and green marble
Rise above a haunting, dead gray horizon

When chance became in favor of life
When justice   favored by the arc of history

Took us all to the heights   to that mountain top
From where we saw our home
As just one small place amid a terrible, vast and dark cold
As had us then regard one another

With a perspective that has made all the difference
And which yet, plays out the world over

Bringing us toward peace!

Those hunting spiders
Between the chard and squash
No earwigs last night.

How I do weeding –
Dig them up carefully
Replant in the wild zone.

A Place Called Home

We had to come about on our journey to find a home
Out here where the roads are few and far between,
We were in a mood to chat on and on
So, only after some hours and miles
Did we see the odometer's evidence
Slowly turn over into proof
Advising us that somewhere, somehow, we missed a turn.

We stopped for a break, a look at the map
And this time we were careful.
We opted to try a side road that was, hopefully, a shortcut,
Soon after as we topped a rise
We saw, in the distance, a copse of tall oak trees
They were stately and impressive.
And were quite the anomaly in this semi arid region.
They became a conversation starter.
We speculated, as we got closer.
And made out a small orchard, too.
So we began to slow as we drew near.
We pulled into the driveway and slowed to a stop,
There, set neatly amid the collection of oaks
Was a stately single story adobe with a red tiled roof.

The building was old, I could tell. The walls were thick.
We really wanted directions and so we drove in.
As she knocked I peered in a window.
Sure enough the sills were a almost a foot wide
On both sides of the pane.
The outer was slanted for run off;
The inner had been tiled for use as a shelf.
The tiles had been painted by children, or so it seemed.

This place was a big, old, and wasn't to be considered,
We knew that but, like I said, we'd made a wrong turn

And this was as good a place as any for getting directions.
A man came to the door acting
Surprised but very welcoming
He'd just put place up for sale, not a half an hour ago.
And thought we were the first comers
We'd had no idea, of course, and laughed at the coincidence,
Told him our bit of a story
But he couldn't figure, from what we'd said,
Which place we'd been looking for.
So he invited us in, pulled out some maps
And, as we looked them over, we chatted as folks might
Quietly, about inconsequential things,
He about the weather, the area, some local history and
We about our hometown, careers, and interests.

He offered us lemonade made from his lemons
And we were surely grateful.

He called the agent and left a message.
Meanwhile he invited us to look around, if only to pass time.
My wife liked the backdrop of distant mountains
Fading into the blue,
Their snowy crags and the mists that played upon them too.

Seeing my wife's glance
He allowed that it never got truly cold here
And in the summer, well, it was hot, plain and simple,
But then, that's why the oaks had been planted
In the first place, to keep the place cool
We allowed that we'd noticed
How the oaks shaded the place all around
I ventured you'd only have to worry about heat
When you traveled – and he agreed.
I went up to one of the trees
And commented that they looked pretty old
He rejoined that his family had planted them 210 years ago.

My wife, looking out to the garden
Commented that its placement and design was practical
It was both to the side and out back.
And we talked about what was coming up and he told us he
Grew Indian corn, from seed stock older than the place was
He quickly added that his wife used to keep it up
And from the way he said it we knew she'd passed
We offered condolences and tactfully let him segue.

He and I went off to look at the small orchard.
It had a good mixture of trees, orange, lemon, apple, cherry,
And a good avocado are what I saw right off.
She remained in garden
As we left he told her to look about as she pleased.

There were some smaller trees
Out by what I thought was a guesthouse.
It too was adobe
But with a footing of orange granite, that was roughly hewn.
He explained that it was from the Spanish days.
That his forbearer was the first Anglo in the territory

According to family legend
One of his mother's ancestors saved a young native girl's life
Her family was both thankful and well connected –
After a time the two families intermarried
The little house and the ranch around it
Was a gift that became the original dwelling for his clan
It measured about 25 by 40 but had a full basement
Later on, with more diverse intermarriages,
They became First Nation, Anglo, Spanish, Korean and more
Family tradition had them maintain the small place
Except for the "new" tile roof, put on a hundred years ago.
The big house, he explained
Had been built by his great great grandfather's family
As we were looking over the small building

I followed him back
She had answered the phone and was laughing
It turned out that his agent and ours were one in the same.
My wife handed him the phone and he took some notes
After he hung up he explained the directions,
Talked about the agent, Mr. Reza, and said the same thing,
 "It's a small world," and then laughed some more.
He made us a quick hand-drawn map
And described the directions
To the place we'd been looking for
We had gotten quite comfortable with each other
And now, well, it was awkward.
She went to freshen up
He and I went outside to the car
So I could look at my map along with his directions.

I was ready to go, but she hadn't come back out.
So we went back inside   I saw her in the pantry
Looking over the built in wooden shelving
And she pointed out the tiled flooring in the kitchen
The phone rang again.
It seemed to be a personal call for him
We excused ourselves and walked around out back.
As we went we talked about the place
It was quite a place really,
But not what we'd had in mind at all … still …
The oaks were appealing,
As was the solidness of the structure
And the settled nature of the place.
So we went out front and stepped away to look it over.
And in our conversation we speculated, caressed really
And appreciated how beautifully simple it was
It was a fascinating house made completely of earth
We broke off our reverie when he reappeared.
Almost embarrassed,
And thanked him and as I shook his hand

I felt his strength and I looked him in the eye
But saw only a misting, a soft look, and
It seemed his eyes were searching mine.
I broke contact, repeating an awkward thanks.

The other place had no calling
Oh, it was modern, nice enough;
A deal we'd have jumped at the day before
But it had nothing intimate or personal
It had been built for investment
And was, in that sense, timeless but, at the same time,
And because of that, completely out of place.
Then, since we still had a part of the late afternoon
And had to get back to our motel
We left, knowing we'd pass by the adobe again.

When we drove up
He was standing by the low stonewall,
Which encircled the place,
Save for the driveway's entrance.
If he was surprised, he didn't show it.
My wife asked if she could freshen up and I
I pretended to be curious about the history of the place
As we talked, I "joined in the fun, put on gloves,
And together we set some large rocks
Back in the wall, slopping cement
Mixed with handfuls river gravel, as we did so.
"You sure do have a unique place."
And he meandered in response, murmuring mostly
As we focused on the task we'd undertaken
Like I say we talked about our families
And though I didn't ask after it, I was sure he said
That he didn't really want to be selling the place
But couldn't hand it down, "Couldn't." I heard him say that.
He mentioned how World War Two,
Korea, and Vietnam had seen to that.

And then, he added wistfully,
"It's been a long time
Since we'd had a Christmas tree in the parlor."
Just then my wife reappeared and called out to us.
And we boys, proudly smiling, showed her our repairs.

As she approached I looked at him
As he seemed to be searching, looking over my face
Or for something to say.

We walked over to a faucet
And began washing our hands;
My wife commented
On the nice way we'd set several of the stones.
Our hands clean, he thanked me with a handshake and
Before we could say anything
And before he was about to walk away
He asked me, us, to wait a minute.
We watched him limp to a shed,
Put away the tools and close its latch.
Before he turned around to face us again
I saw his life here,
In those brief, clipped, comments
The centuries of family rooted
How this denouement— so unexpectedly simple
Consisting as it does of a last few precious hours
Spent replacing stones, sweeping the flagstone path,
Or tending the garden.
We both saw him and thought about his story,
On a quiet ordinary day, we came to an understanding
Of his completely long perspective, his feelings, or
How his attitude toward his home had become just as permanent
As his attitude toward the strangers
Who would buy all he knew of
Or cared about in this world.

Good News

I want some good news people
No, not that "born-again"
Bible humping bullpucky you've heard tell of   nope
I want good news – and not just for a minute here or there
Like you get during a KPFA fundraiser
Not what you get on Faux News during a slow day
No, by God, I want the real deal
I want a whole workweek stuffed full of it
With each book-ending weekend fit to bursting
I want to turn on the TV and feel good
And feel good every time I think about anything I think of
And be double-dipped, full up, schmeared, in good news
I tell you I want to look at the sky
And not think about "chem-trail" conspiracies
I want to feel the wind in my hair
Without wondering if toxic crap is being carried along in it
From the sewers of India, China's deserts, or Japan's nukes
I want to wake up, turn on NPR and hear wonderful things
Expanding forests and glaciers along with fish populations
Safe cell phones that pay YOU to use them
Free food being given out, rent reductions running rampant
And the president giving back trillions to the people,
Closing Guantanamo, giving up on nuclear power,
Bringing troops home from Iraq, Afghanistan, Yemen, Bahrain,
Oman, Egypt, Jordan, Lebanon, Turkey, Iran, Kazakhstan,
Balochistan, Turkmenistan, Venezuela, Colombia, all 123
I want to hear him go on about perp-walking Bush
And his whole suffering ass-hole crew
Placing a stay on all that rim-jobbing bunghumper did
That prisons are being shuttered
Because millions of people decide to care for each other
That once godless heathen multinationals are hiring people
Because they're bringing rock solid, plan retirement on 'em
God blessed union jobs to the USA – by the millions

I want to hear about green houses, green cars, green factories,
Green makeup, green jobs, and
A greening self-sustaining world
I want to hear how every person entering the job market
Saying the same ding-dong thing, "Gee, I don't know
Which one of all these jobs do I want?" AND
"Say, why don't you CEO's take numbers for crissakes!"
And, mind you, I want good news on every frickin' day
I want to hear how millions are giving up cigarettes
Taking up Pilates, volunteering for charity work
That everyone has two chickens in every pot
A good, well-built, American car in every garage
And by that I mean one that gets 500 miles per fuel up,
Takes a 50 mile an hour head-on crash with no damage
Or injury to its passengers, is "green"
Lasts as long as you frickin' want to keep it
And gets free tune-ups, brake jobs and tires as you own it
I want scenic passenger trains to make a comeback
How scientists are being listened to   Hello!!!
Got global warming on the run
Replaced oil, coal, nuclear power and natural gas
Found a way to prevent alcoholism
Using the cures for cancer that we already have
And have begun to terra-form the Earth for God's sake

I want to hear day after day of good news
So that by the time the fourth day dawns
I'll see what life's like in a world that makes sense
So that I'll be looking forward to the next blessed day
So that I'll be glad to wake up
Donate to good causes, of which there'll be thousands,
And every one will be doing well thank you very much
I want all the guns in the world to be turned in
Broken up and melted down to make – anything else!
I want to hear that every soldier, intel wonk, officer

Commando or insurgent
Has renounced violence and is getting busy
Building shelters, planting trees, cleaning beaches
Counseling the hopeless, caring for the needy
Handing out bread, bringing in water
Giving emergency care to the destitute
Rescuing cats from trees and kissing babies
I wanna see them all get busy
Fixing every leaky toilet, broken window, noisy refrigerator, and
Ding-blasted pothole in the known universe – and that they are
Working with farmers to grow more food unlocking potential,
Opening floodgates applying bandages, splints
And helping, helping, helping!

I want banksters making microloans, giving grants
Hear that defense departments have been shut down!
That research and development funding
Is allocated to making better computers
Cars, planes, trains, tractors, shoes, lights, batteries, houses,
Farms, cities, colleges, schools, basketball, and food courts!

I want to hear about better understanding
Between religions, races, politicians, and historical enemies
I want to hear about borders being erased,
Hatreds evaporating,
Ignorance giving way   reason running rampant
And every form of love
Being accepted by everyone EVERYWHERE!

By God, I want a week of such good news
As people have never ever, ever, EVER had

So when I go outside
And get my free cup of fair trade,
Organic, sustainable coffee
And an organic "everything" bagel

Everyone will be walking about more than a bit dazed
More than a bit confused
But each and every one will be happy, happy, happy!

Hallelujah

Hallelujah!
Brothers and sisters, but I yearn, dream, and pray
For such a week
I say I want a week of good news
A flood, an ocean, a sky full of wonders

So that every memory of this time;
This horrific, festering butt hole
This stupid-assed, jack-shit, fucked up,
Universally acclaimed
And God awful world of unholy, rank, fulminating
Pustulant oozing scabs …

Is gone.

I say I want a week of good news, my friends
I say, I want a week of such good news
That glory unbounded I know
I say, I just know,
We all want to see!

Three

Considerations

Answering Silly Questions

I am circular
Making my rounds
Going with the flow
Winding up back where I started from
After reaching the ends
Which mystified the means … I mean
I turn back to reflect
Only to see the futures' mirrored
In the looking glass behind me – then
Which then be seen for what it is
An ephemeral glimpse
No more substantial
Than an idle thoughts passing

I am the shape
Of wind motioning branches
The unseen currents
In what appears to be a cool, still pond
Reflecting only the sky

I am the voice of memories
The sweet warm murmuring muse,
The silence of second-guessing,
Or a glimpse of insight

I am that which has
Four legs in the morning
Two in the afternoon
And three at night
Simply   I am the song
Whispered by the leaves of corn
In summer
The polyrhythm of the dandelion's tumbling up
Into the sky … disappearing into background clouds

The strains of a creek's crusting over
In winter
The crocus in the frost
And the wearing away
Of mountains
Through the blink of seasons

I am the loneliest number
In the simplest equation
Identifying everything
And signifying nothing
I can be added to
Everything and subtracted
From nothing
All while remaining unchanged
Undifferentiated and unappreciated

I am a classic
With old style lines
A sturdy frame, new grillwork
And I still have plenty of miles
Both on the odometer and yet to go
I've been maintained
And through the touch ups
Can still be seen for what I am
While the clever or knowing person
Could determine those accidents
If they look
And though I am built for comfort
I can still floor it and put on speed

I am a comfortable sofa
If I were to be any piece of furniture at all
Or an end table received for free, from a friend
And with nothing much wrong
Well, maybe it just needs a touch up … and

A cleaning for sure
Then it could be duded up
Made into a show piece
Fit for someone's Sunday parlor,
A prop for a struggling theatre group,
Something to be resold at a garage sale when you move on

I am a jar of sprouts
Fresh, homemade,
Cheap, to be sure,
Healthy,
And made to be given away

I would be a harmonica
Simple to play
Easily hidden
And as complex as you might like

I am in the heart of any lover
The soul of any peacemaker
The mind of any tinker

I am imagination's fire
And the twinkle in an eye

I would be an old oak tree,
Respected by the people who celebrate beneath it
And I would not be alone
For my forest would be fast by
And I would provide for those temporal beings
Both food and shelter
Because I am giving,
Nurturing,
Kind, and helpful
For I cannot help myself
For being the what that I am

I am unafraid
Of death
And so I am unafraid of everything
For I know that all fear
Is simply a fear of death however disguised

Behind my eyes
Is a universe,
Galaxies of worlds,
Where my ancestors roamed
Where I go whenever I reflect
Between each thought
Each pulse of my being
I transcend the appearance I am beheld by
My love is the painted landscapes and
Misty vistas of worlds without end
The music of the heavenly spheres
And the symphony of all there is

You Mustn't Be Afraid Of Death.

What is death
If not graceful   quiet   a peaceful singularity
Where the eternal and the infinite   kiss

Now, I know you must know passion, my friends
How the burning heart
Turns the soul   bends the mind
And sweats out that body   uh-huh
I know you know what I'm talkin' 'bout

And so you think of death as a loss
But it's more
It IS "all that" and then some

Think about it; death does not harm you
Life does that   believe you me
Can I have an "Amen"?

Death delivers you
From the suffering flesh
The tortures of reason
The cold steel chains of logic
And the binding wrap
Of self-designed deceit, conceits, and illusions

Death holds nothing to fear
That's what life is for
Death is not cruel nor is it painful
Nope   those are both life's work too
And you know I'm right
Consider the worst: death is nothing more
Than nothing more
And if it's not
If you're into, say, reincarnation

Well, take everything I say here
And multiply it 500 times
Death is easy   anyone can do it   once
Afterwards you won't have to worry
You'll get used to it
After awhile you'll have no choice   after awhile
You'll see there's nothing to it
It'll be like slippin' into something more comfortable

After leaving that so called life you left behind
So you mustn't be afraid of death
Doesn't just about everyone say
That's when you get to meet your maker
Wouldn't you want to do that   I mean at least once?
Say everything you want to say
Ask all those questions?

Afraid of death?
Don't be foolish
There is no dark grave for the deathless soul
One filled with light;
Happily dwelling in a shimmering world
Set in a heavenly fire-scape of glory
And blissful with love

Such foreknowledge dissuades one from fearing death
Banishes all the mourning and abiding regrets
And secures a peace no bitterness can touch
Beyond the reach of malice
There is nothing but joy

Only the lost and forgetful
Dwell in death's sorrows my friend
Which is why I say it
In this life
Death should be the least of your worries!

Where is your heart?
Right here   right now?
This   very   moment …
You know what I mean
Not just the percussive muscular motions
Marking your moment to moment measures
But   that singular, most intimate part
Which knows   every   little   thing
Yes   the unending part
And how it takes you   and where it takes you
And why   why   you go along
With its intimate emotive   feelings of
That's the ticket … where is your heart
When you dearly miss its peace?
When you cannot take its pain any longer
And you beg it to please
Please   just   stop   the ache
That comes   as steadily on
As each   regrettable beat   does
Bringing up memories that come   only to go
With each and every   breath
As each hope or   wish   follows on   yes
Where   is your heart tonight?
What is it about?   What   are its intentions?
How does it figure in your life?
And what plans do you have for it?
How do you hold it dear?
How do you protect it?
And what   what does it want of you
What is it always   asking?
So   where is your heart   tonight
Ladies and gentlemen?
Where … would you have it be?
What does   it   wish?   and why   why do you ever
Let it play   second fiddle
To anything else?

202

Four

One Thing Leads to Another

The Irish Sieve

By what light may a great poem be recognized?
What are its telling marks, signs or signification?

Let us consider the common indicators:
The manner of its reception by audience, say,
Their laughter, knowing nods, murmurs and,
Of course, the approbations
Perhaps, but it can't only be those
For, were it so, one would, in every café, salon or saloon
Hear the flow of immortal words
Be inundated with phrases that quicken the heart
Drawn along by stanzas which take centuries in their stride
All while each and every word
Tingles on the poet's trembling ardent lips
Even as their breathy rhythms
Embody temptation and titillate
While the lusty denizens of the den,
In curious love, are rapt, enthralled and lick their lips
As they covet each dear utterance, as were they God's own.

So, no, it could not just be that
And one can see it readily enough –
Fickle applause compliments twinkling eyes, facial jests
The actor's pose or gesticulation … the ample actress
It rewards simple humor, poor puns
And easy contemporary reference
Even the banal or rude –
If such be wrapped in the current style –
And while I admit such works provide relief
Or even temporal worth
Divorced of those simple affectations,
Poetry of this kind is suffered only and remains truly small;
Even were it to be chiseled in stone
And how could greatness hinge on subject matter alone

For grand themes such as love, war and freedom
Can be mean
And altogether wanting – leave it to a poor poet
To make the extraordinary – ordinary and,
Contrariwise, to genius
For elevation of the ordinary … the fly's buzz
The lark's singing over the sullen earth – a wheelbarrow
Or dewy plums to warrant eternal laurels

I trust you'll agree it couldn't simply be a poem's length
Or a poet's vocal prowess
For not only does the latter fail in print
I have been put to sleep by stentorian odes, which march on
With certitude toward a notch mark on a distant horizon
While, moments later,
Been utterly ravished by a mere 17 syllables …
Whispered
Or shaken by a few simple quatrains
Of a Persian bard centuries dead

While there are works that seep in through the senses
Roil emotions and precipitate passion
Those that prompt precious pearly tears
Yet, however moving,
Simply personal journeys may well distract from
Rather than raise up a yearning for works of pure mind,
The appreciation of inspiration,
And excite the exquisite thirst for more of that vintage,
For which only a poet is both brewer of and repository of,
So, a great poem must do more than simply root at the heart
If it does not delve into its recessional deeps
Wrestle the soul from its precious keep
And wring it out for all it's worth –
Such poems can still miss the long mark
Some say a great poem is one published and widely read
Which becomes part-and-parcel to its time

As it informs, clarifies or well becomes the zeitgeist
Is found acceptable, even to the millions,
Who may then quote parts without knowing their source
Yes, this is closer, for many would say
Such a poem would be great,
For its merits elevate it over others
Which do not do that kind of justice
And fairness to the word
Yet, all things considered, it may still not be great
For while such indicates
The length and breadth of a great poem,
Providing society with value – it may still be ordinary

If that poem does have its own voice,
Is so intimate with humanity
That it's whisper is not lost to time,
If it sings with the living chorus
Keeping ever alive as the poet was when first it was penned
Then,
Then we are closer still,
For such a work would have no limit
Would ring throughout the ages harboring vitality,
Which brings us then to a singular test,
One as dynamic as it is unforgiving ... if not fair:

A poem must have flight ... no ...
Soar into the celestial fields,
So, that by hailing its presence,
The people are drawn to a new perspective
A great vision or dream!
And it wouldn't matter if the author was unknown
Or if his people and world – have long been dust
And yes,
Even some of the simplest of poems
Could meet this requirement
Though they be no more than a loving portrait,

A vibrant reflection of their birthplace
Or crafted as a messenger, harbinger, time capsule
For those for whom it is intended,
Whether for a time, an age, or beyond such conditions
Which brings us to a paradox in this whole consideration

That we cannot recognize a great poem
Cannot see what it will become with time and grace
Cannot be its only audience, critics, or fans
Cannot be amongst those
Who'll live better for its influence upon their forebears
Those whose history is richer for its resource
Or those who grew up entranced by its magic
And have fallen so in love with it
So as to give it their breath and passion

It is not possible for a poem of this day, however favored,
To have sea of gazing eyes reflecting in its long glory
The Great Mansion has not reverberated with its musing
It has not yet survived the cold passage of time –
Whose finality gleans the germ from the husk, hull, or chaff
We all know that as humankind
Ever needs to refine their truth,
To determine who they are,
So will they plumb the secrets of their past
Hoping to unravel the puzzle of what they call the present.
They'll seek ancestral troves to find out who they really are
And a great poem will allow them this boon

The future being what it is
We cannot see any poem, as they will
We can say that it may well be seen
In ways we cannot hope to understand
Because we are in what they'd call the past
Just as a fish assumes its sea, as it were
So odds are a great poem will be unrecognized in its time

Even the masters of language,
Those who chronicle poetic efforts,
The academics, critics, or poets themselves
All may fail to see it, and easily so!

As for poets, I hold that they are the most blind of all
For the poetic voice is rare
It is a sense that becomes art … when they embody it
Each of them has an appreciation for their fellow traveler
Which is altogether dear – and sweet enough to cry for,
Nonetheless, they are blind for all that

Lost, joyously in love, they cherish each other's hearts
Finding, in each poem,
A sincere and loving gesture to the muse
Even in works meant for an audience of one
A great poem is, of course,
A product of both its time and place
As well as of no time or place
It is a corpus, which lives
Taking the life of the poet along with it
And so it takes the meaning of life itself … with it

In such a poem, one finds the heart of the matter
Of all matter and for all time
So that you, dear reader, may visit that sphere
The lofty firmament of the soul
Where great poems call and echo
As they become, even as life itself is
Both momentary and transcendent
While expressing a yearning, borne of itself, to be free
Of all fetters, all forms or fashionings

The Passing Of Brady's Fart

On a moonless Carrigallen eve
When the fairy's wind blew just right
There was a hissing, burning vent
Hardly audible in the wee of the night
But a pack of starveling dogs were scattered off;
They ran away howling
And the legendary Brady it was
Who breached that mighty fouling
They say he burst his breeches along the inseam
And verily through
That although he was outside he left the scene,
Seeking fresh air too
Yea, friends, this was a ghastly break of wind,
Horrifically passed
So that even in the dark of night, drunk, alone,
He was somberly put aghast

And it was this that started a tale,
Which has not yet met its ends
For to this day there lingers a trail
Amongst both his foes and friends.
The mild wind carried the filthy air
Straight along the street
Where it startled cats, interrupting
Even those in a fevered humping heat
Then too, and not far away, some drunken brutes
Got into one hell of a brawl
As each accused the others of disbursing such a waft,
As made their skins crawl
Their clamor awakened the good people
Slumbering abed in houses there
Who, with curious eyes, opened windows
But then couldn't believe the air
Several sickened loosing their dinners into the street,

Children they cried
Old man Shannon he woke up, took a sniff,
Had a heart attack, and died
The McEnroy's, as ever, found in it an excuse,
As if they needed one that night,
To begin, then and there, and proudly,
A bitter, loud domestic fight
Still confused the howling dogs,
Came back down that same poor street.
And yes they and brawlers both tangled
As they all chanced to meet.
This chaos startled some nearby cattle in a pen
And then the sheep.
And these, for want of good air, trod over the stakes
And so escaped their keep.

The rioting beasts crashed a near barn
And brought down its loft to rout
Harbored lovers, one pair, who fell, it is said,
Still joined in their sweet redoubt
Who tried in vain to make safe their escape
From that splintered pile
Yet were discovered on their way to their respective beds
Well apart by a mile
Yes, that foul wind set cruel fate
Against their fervent desire
As disheveled and in mental tumult,
Their disjointed alibi's lit suspicions' fire
Far too many mentioned seeing them out
On that unholy night
And before it was done both came to rue the relations
Which thereby came to light

Her twin sister, there too, also furtive, in the barn
Was as well, in delicate repose
And one can only imagine her thoughts

When she gnashed down, we suppose
To sever her dearest's relation,
Which wriggled under her very nose
Leaving him but a bitter root,
Which would never more enjoy delicate flows
Oh, he is among the village still;
For he came through it whole other ways
But she suffered a gangrenous leg
That lingered on for many days
And, when the truth came out, her father took it up
And hung it out to dry
One can still see what's left, her foot,
For it's on his mantle withered and dry.

And still she'll prattle bemoaning bitter fate,
To her sister face to face
For they were twins,
Both conniving to marry into a higher place.
They both worked up their manger trap
Each in their own little head
Yet, their dearly laid plans went so far awry
That each found she'd gotten the wrong man to bed
Most hold it was either not meant to be, nor undone,
And few know the whole part
Of all that passed within in that failing barn
On the night of Brady's Fart.
What happened with the commotion
Was something a bit wilder we fear
As families, beasts, and fowl brawled
On the commons so dark and drear

The noise was heard at McGee's Pub
Causing him to wake and horribly curse
His wife, a Lynch no less, took up the struggle
And back talked him in verse
There were many who came to quell this cacophonic din

But soon all in this wonderful hamlet
Were full tilt given over to commodious riot
Well, what do you think, but a cellar
Was broken out for its barrels of brew
These and some dark bottles were brought to the scene
And enlivened it too
There was dancing, and music to boot
For those taking a break from the brawl
And no one, mind, not even Brady,
Really knew what had started it all

No bedlam, no soccer game's loss,
No mad monk at the cathedral bell
No, nothing save opposing forces at bitter war
Could raise such riotous hell
Whiskey was looted, maidens screamed
While men carried off livestock and then
Police arrived, just after three,
But it didn't quiet down until half past ten
As usual, the city papers, out the next day,
Tried to get it down a'right
But couldn't explain how some old roughs
And street dogs had gotten into a fight.
Or how farm animals, neighbors
And whole town had just been drawn right in.
They hailed it as proof that, ironically for the Irish,
Drinking must be a sin.

Yes, you know the story now,
Though you'd never think such a hullabaloo
Would arise on a night
When the gentle southern fairy winds blew
Or how unintended consequences followed
After a twitching thing fell out a flue
To die in Brady's bubbling pot
Cabbage, onion, and buttered garlic stew.

212

Five

Insights and Visions

How she holds me
With all encompassing compassion
Her vaulting great womb
Her … sky of jet
Vast deep and spectacular
Glistening with galaxies

How she holds me
In her wondrous bright blue gaze
All above and round about
As the world faces her sovereign's blaze

How she holds me   in our valley
Between these ridgelines
Their silhouettes … her profiles   yes!
Breathe deep the gathering gloom
And scent into the wind touching my face
As fascinating changes
Wash the horizons with blush

How she holds me
The reflection my lover's eyes
The sparkle there … her light
Before me … upon me

How she holds me
In the warmth of her hands
In her heart and with nary a whisper
From the smile in her words

How   she holds
Me   within our hearts
Upon our world
Forever and ever … on and on …
How – she holds me

What Makes Me Smile?

Sometimes   sunshine
On my shoulder makes me happy
On a warm day
As a cool breeze
Comes down the way
Rustling the sidewalk's leaves
As I stroll along shushing them aside
As if I've nothing better to do   have no plans
And am at ease

But today I smiled when I thought about the garden
How the spinach is doing,
If I'll pick those strawberries,
Trim the roses back or cut a few blossoms ,
Maybe turn over compost,
Just to watch the bugs,
Water a bit and enjoy the rainbows in the arc of water
As it glistens before it settles into darkening soil

I smile as rough up the soil
Keeping an eye out for those hunting spiders
Giving them a sure free pass from trowel or claw

I smile when I check the blush on the tomatoes
Or as I stand and stretch to pause from it all
As the sun brightens
Or as I sit quietly in a garden chair
Maybe as I look forward to a nap,
A good afternoon snooze even
With the windows wide open
And fresh air wafting in as birds call

I smile
As I take time to empty concerns

Yes, that's one time I smile

I smile when I sing,
Or talk with a friend

I also smile
When my wife comes home
And we greet each other at the door
Because the doorbell is working that day
And we go for a hug or two, or three

When she smiles at me
Or uses one of our many, many nicknames

Or we banter a bit
Give each other the eye
Or a pat on the fanny

Well,

Come to think of it
We smile pretty darned easily at our house
In fact,
We got a whole lotta smilin' going on

Oh yeah …

Sufi Camp Haiku

Walking up the grade
of packed drying mud, distracted
by my thoughts and slipping –

I set to flight coveys
in the grasses and foliage
at either hand.

Small grey birds
with white under wings
flutter to safety.

Later, crows call
and then jays
amid redwoods.

Laughter passes through the canopy
And a refreshing breeze –
Smiling

I can't begin
to write them all –
Redwood's Haiku!

The dandelion
drifts under dapples blinking
hardly a breath of air.

Harp's tell in the dell.
Our storied music memoirs –
We both turn give a wink

Through the redwood's screen,
 a strange circle of colors:
  Sufis in the light.

All up in a heat!
  Stomping with Ram many times –
    Many times to come.

Light plays about,
  Upon a strand of web,
    Its prisms slip, side.

Feet coated with dust,
faces to the sun, mouths wide,
circling singers praise!

A blindfold on him,
this jackass standing quite still
in the new pasture.

Frame and backdrop
all of redwoods, their laughter
though, brings me to glance.

100 yards, off
drifting – the bright down feather
high over the pond.

Myriad motes
catch light.   Still, the tiny insect's
point of blurred wings.

The Drying Rack

How does love begin?
And how long does it take –
To get from the unknown there to a very well known here?

In my case, it's taken about a billion seconds;
You see, there was once sunshine on a cloudy day,
A cancelled date, and an idle decision to turn a corner
And it was that little instant,
Which was followed by
All those other instants,
Until I arrived at today's, this evening's.
When I heard simple sounds from the kitchen.

There was running water,
A couple clatters, soft of course, from the rack –
It sounded as if it was a saucepan's lid
Settling into its angle of repose,
Sparkling glasses tapping my old mug or
One of our "moon bowls."

Really, any of things she set with up care
Which, by chance and physics,
Over time, suffered subtle readjustments
As they shifted from arrangement into rearrangement.
Could contribute to this jazzy composition.
As the dripping sculpture in the drying rack
Continued to sound she began to hum
An elder song we both love.
Then, came a light tapping,
As if a conductor signaled intent
There followed a moment of silence –
As if a baton was raised.
This brought her kindness to mind and
Her fascinating musical style … then …

As I was about to call out,
She, for whatever reason asked something,
Which, because the water was running,
And she was in another room,
And I was multi-tasking,
I didn't hear completely –
So I asked her to repeat it   and she said,

"How come you didn't hear me the first time?"

And I said, "Oh, I'm sorry; I couldn't …"
Now, what I was really doing
Was trying to think up some clever response
That would say something very old to us
Yet in a very, very new at the same time.

So there was a pause.

I guessed she was waiting, so I added,
"Well, I wanted to say, more exactly, I mean …"

"That you love me!" The smile in her voice – clear as a bell,
"In all my mysterious ways, and for all that I do!"

Another pause followed; I added, "And for all that you are …"

"And more!" She rejoined.

And more, indeed!
What with a billion seconds or so and counting
We still cast our spells
Upon one another
For the simple joy of it!

Airy fields Of Green

I will call to you
As you'll call to me
When you've become departed
And I'll say what's true
How our love's still new
Though you lay beneath the green

Oh it's always clear
When true love is here
That it opens what we started
'Neath cloud's finery
Spent in felicity
Soft upon the downs of dreams

And when – still here are we
Where we danced happily
As we opened into time
Then took to trails of fate
O'er the hills in rhyme
To the glistening spring of joy!

And yes, I will call to you
As you'll call to me
When we've become departed
And we'll say we're true
To our love – still new
Though I with you
Lay – beneath the green

This is a most recent photo, taken at Ocean Beach, near to our special 30th anniversary,

Yes! Give this book away!

When you give this book away, please initial it here, and indicate where and when you handed it off. I'd like these to meander the world over to perhaps migrate back to San Francisco as kind of message in a bottle. I look forward to its MUNI debut, seeing it on someone's bookshelf, or at a garage sale.

Initials   City   Date

_____

_____

_____

_____

_____

_____

_____

_____

_____

_____

224

_____

_____

_____

_____

_____

_____

_____

_____

_____

_____

_____

_____

Once this page is full, use any other page – go for it!